'*Now, Lead Others* is a fantastic follow on from *Yourself*. Delivered through an easy to follow conversation between friends, this book delivers numerous leadership concepts and tools in an easy to absorb, yet thought provoking way. I found myself reflecting and considering my own leadership style constantly throughout the story. A must have book for anyone leading or seeking to lead others.'

David Morrison

CEO, Thankyou Payroll

Co-owner DoGoodJobs.co.nz

'*Now, Lead Others* by Cillín Hearns is an exceptional example of artful storytelling delivering rich insights of essential leadership principles. Cillín masterfully weaves a narrative around a crucial toolset of leadership strategies which will enhance the qualities of any leader. Cillín's approach will help you to additionally delve deep into the core aspects of effective team dynamics, fostering any leader's ability to unleash their potential and enhancing any leader's journey towards facilitating harmonious team management – and delivering the exceptional performance that comes from that. *Now, Lead Others* is more than a sequel to Cillín's first book; it is a crucial companion in anyone's leadership library, empowering them to build and facilitate transformative dynamics within their teams.'

Darcy Mellsop

Director, ci lab

Author of *Unleashing the Improvement Mindset*

'I really don't know how he did it. Cillín has managed to pack an enormous amount of key leadership thinking and learnings into this book. Cillín's ability to weave a great tale around what might otherwise be fairly dry management thinking has made this a book worth owning and reading. I not only thoroughly enjoyed the storyline, but found myself being drawn into the conversations between the main characters as they explored many aspects of applying leadership theory. His use of anecdotes to describe key concepts can only come from experience.

I think this is a book that you would use to dive back into again and again as it has a wealth of material that is completely relevant to the world of work and life that we live in today. If you are like me and can never quite remember those 4 or 5 key points, this will set you back on track.'

Terry McCaul

CEO, Royal NZ College of General Practitioners

CFHRINZ; AFIMNZ; MBA

'*Now, Lead Others* cleverly condenses key leadership concepts into a clear and engaging format. I was hooked from the start, and the practical examples made it easy to see how these ideas could be applied in my own day-to-day work. Whether you're aiming to build a high-performing team or simply become a more effective leader, Now, Lead Others offers invaluable insights and actionable strategies. Highly recommended!'

Emma Parker

Principal Leadership Advisor, Civil Aviation Authority

'The leadership framework in *Now, Lead Others* is built on decades of solid leadership theory that has been skilfully adapted for our modern world. Please, enjoy the story, let yourself be open to new ways of thinking about leadership, and apply what you have learned in work and at home.'

David Keane, PhD

Author of *The Art of Deliberate Success*

'Leadership books can be a chore sometimes but this one was engaging and easy to read, with the same humour and sense of mischief Cillín brought in his first book. However, *Now, Lead Others* is different, it's a story of adventure. I found the book took me on a personal journey of reflection, intrigue and excitement, eager to put the lessons learnt into action.'

Kirstie Knowles

Director, Department of Conservation

Also by Cillín Hearns:

First, Lead Yourself

Now, Lead Others

Practical Tools and Insights on How to Build

High Performing Teams

Cillín Hearns

The web addresses referenced in this book were live and correct at the time of the book's publication but may be subject to change. Every effort has been made to trace (and seek permission for use of) the original source material used within this book. Where the attempt has been unsuccessful, the publisher would be pleased to hear from the author/publisher to rectify any omission.

Hearns, Cillín

Now, lead others: Practical tools and insights on how to build high performing teams / Cillín Hearns.

Pages cm

Includes bibliographical references.

ISBN 978-0-473-71514-4

A catalogue record for this book is available from the National Library of New Zealand.

To my mother, Ann.

Thank you for being the original compass in my life and for guiding me through life's storms.

Contents

Foreword   *xxiii*

The End   1

The Wicklow Mountains   7

The Plan   17

The First Lesson   25

The Art of Delegation   31

The Visionary   45

The Coach   61

The Affiliate   73

The Flash of Light   89

The Connection   99

The Commander   103

The Debrief   111

The Democrat   117

The Order   129

The Most Important Thing   141

The Reason We're In Business 151

The Three Outcomes 157

The Art of Giving Feedback 165

The Millennials 173

The Dream 177

The Man From Cork 185

The Beginning 193

The Interview 195

Epilogue 199

Bibliography 233

About the Author 237

Foreword

The Canadian musician Loreena McKennitt wrote a song with the title *The Dark Night of the Soul,* which is on her album *The Mask and the Mirror.*

A few years ago, I was fortunate to be at a concert where she sang the song. It was an evening I will never forget. That night, the stage was completely dark except for a small candle lighting Loreena's face.

In her perfect and clear soprano voice, she beautifully unfolded *The Dark Night of the Soul,* which described a crisis of faith or a difficult, painful period, we sometimes experience in life.

The dark night is a time of reflective soul searching where some of our most basic assumptions about life come under the spotlight.

The philosopher Joseph Campbell writes that, "The dark night of the soul comes just before revelation. When everything is lost, and all seems darkness, then comes the new life and all that is needed".

Reading Cillín's brilliant book, I was reminded of dark night of the soul moments many of us experience as we grow and mature in our leadership journey. Perhaps what has worked well for us in the past is no longer serving us. Perhaps we need a re-think.

What I love about Cillín's book is how he gently takes us by the hand as we examine our own leadership styles. We can all relate to the key character in the book — Nathan — as he experiences his own dark night, learns about himself and confronts some home truths. There is a Nathan in all of us and Cillín has found a clever way to find him.

The leadership framework in *Now, Lead Others* is built on decades of solid leadership theory that has been skilfully adapted for our modern world. Please, enjoy the story, let yourself be open to new ways of thinking about leadership, and apply what you have learnt in work and at home.

David Keane, PhD

Author of *The Art of Deliberate Success*

The End

It'll be easier in the morning.

Nathan shifted uncomfortably in the seat. It was a smaller car than he was used to driving. It was just past 6 p.m. and the news spoke of a turbulent weather front coming in across the country — expect heavy wind and rain in some parts, it said. Turbulent … that sounded exactly how he'd describe his own life at the moment. How the situation could change from sunny and clear skies to unpredictable and fucking turbulent so quickly. It was a long time since he'd been back in Ireland and even though his memory had faded a little the familiarity of the road opened up to him. He anticipated the large green sign for Blanchardstown that would signify his turn-off. He couldn't shake the thought; how could life become so unsatisfactory so quickly? The sign came into view and he took the off-ramp. He found himself mouthing the words to the song playing on the radio. The Hothouse Flowers … it occurred to him how much he missed the

Irish bands. The words washed over him. They lamented a lonely night with promises of a brighter morning.

The weather, the lyrics — it was all too much but one thing was for sure. It certainly wouldn't be easier in the morning. He'd be facing a thirty-six hour flight back to New Zealand, back to all the problems he got a reprieve from when the call came through.

It took him a moment to recognise the house. The front garden was overgrown, the iron gate was rusted and hanging off its hinges. He saw Fionn's Toyota Prius, which confirmed he was in the right place. How long had it been? Easily eight years. He stepped out in the darkening sky and pulled up his collar against the drizzle. Tonight would be a good night. He hadn't seen the lads in such a long time; a few beers, a few laughs. He pushed down the negativity and pressed the doorbell. The door swung open with energy and Nathan was greeted with a big smile and a hug.

'Come on in. I'll just be a couple of minutes getting the folks comfortable for the night. Pop your head in and say hello.'

Fionn walked through the door to the sitting room, and Nathan, as requested, popped his head in. His senses were hit by the smell of dust and sickness. Fionn's parents had been unwell for a long time. They rarely left the house, and with his sister living in a separate part of the country, he spent every spare moment he had looking after them.

'Hello, Mr and Mrs O'Reilly,' Nathan said. They looked up from watching the television.

'Ah, how're ye, Nate?'

'I'm great, thanks,' he replied. 'It's great to see you both looking so well.'

'Ah, go on outta dat,' Mrs O'Reilly scoffed. 'Sure we can hardly wipe our own arses these days.' The Dublin humour always brought a smile to his face. 'Come're, Nate. We were very sorry to hear about your da. How's your ma doin'?'

'Oh, she's grand. She has the whole family around her. She'll be okay—.'

'Right,' interrupted Fionn. 'Let's get you both settled in for the night.' He turned to Nathan. 'Pop across the hall, I won't be long.'

Nathan nodded. 'It's nice to see you both again, Mr and Mrs O'Reilly.'

'Right so, Nate.' Their eyes had already returned to the television.

Nathan closed the door and made his way to the room across the hall. Stepping across the threshold was like stepping back in time — nothing had changed. This was the room they all used to hang out in when they were at Fionn's place. The carpet was threadbare, but the rest of the room was untouched — the room that time forgot. The centrepiece of the room was a dilapidated sofa facing the large and outdated television screen. Between the two sat a small table for beers or feet, or as was evident by the stains on the carpet, both at the same time. At the back of the room was a wall of movies — DVDs and video cassettes. Fionn loved his movie collection, but judging from the build-up of dust, hadn't indulged in a movie night in quite a while.

To the left of the door was a coat rack with hangers full of mountaineering coats, ropes, and hats. One glove stuck out of the pocket of one of the coats as if to say hi and the other lay lifeless on a large yellow North Face bag full to the brim. On either side of the bag was a pair of hill-walking boots with laces open and tongues out. Nathan didn't know how Fionn fitted it all in. Two young kids, ailing parents, full-time job and he volunteered for mountain rescue.

A photograph on the mantelpiece above the fireplace caught Nathan's eye. He picked up the heavy red frame and smiled as the memories came flooding back. In his hands he held the last picture of the lads together at the same time. Fionn was wearing a dark pinstriped suit with a pink tie. Hugo was in a white shirt stretched over his muscular frame. Buttons were open at the neck and the knot on his red tie was loose and hung halfway down his chest. Nathan stood in the middle wearing a golden waistcoat, a white shirt with cufflinks and a red cravat, with a newly placed ring on his left hand. They used to joke how they were all the same height as one another. Nathan never believed this to be true. He always thought he was shorter but looking at the photograph now, it was true; there was barely a centimetre difference. The smiles were wide and spoke of a time without cares, a time without worries. *A different time to now. How did it all go horribly wrong?* That thought again. It was like a virus that kept pulling him back to a world he couldn't escape — a world of pain and uncertainty. He sat heavily on the sofa and dropped his head in his hands.

'Fuckers,' he muttered to himself. Life would be so much easier if he hadn't inherited such a bunch of fuckers.

Part of him wanted to tell Fionn all about it. He knew he'd get the support he needed and it would make him feel better — for a while. Another part of him was too embarrassed. He remembered bragging on the phone only three months ago about how he'd scored his dream job. What would he tell him now? Hey, remember that team of software engineers, testers, business analysts and architects I was running? Well guess what? I'm messing it all up. They hate me!

The conversation with Claudia in the Amber Room was fresh in his mind. That's what they called the room, which nobody could book, and that was used for impromptu meetings. Nathan knew now he shouldn't have pushed her so hard. Claudia was a good boss. Months earlier, sitting across from her on the couch in Latitude 44 during their first meeting and being told he got the job really made his day — made his year. The smell of coffee and the chattering of patrons was still fresh in his mind. Claudia was great at making everyone feel special. The team loved Claudia, and Nathan was thrilled to be working for her, and taking over the responsibility of running the team, which would free her up to pursue larger career ambitions. That was three months ago. As he stood in the Amber Room the conversation felt very different. Claudia was always patient and careful with her feedback and Nathan kicked himself for pushing her the way he did, but he couldn't help it. The frustration consumed him almost to breaking point.

'You've got to tell them that they report to me now,' he'd said to her and the words echoed around his skull.

'I can't do that,' she replied.

'You've got to! You've got to tell them that I'm their boss and what I say goes.'

'I can't do that,' Claudia repeated as she tried to remain composed.

'You've got to!' Nathan said yet again.

In the end Claudia became exasperated. 'I can't tell them that because if I do, they'll all quit.'

The look of shock on Nathan's face caused Claudia to instantly regret her words. They both stood there, staring at one another, neither sure of what to do next. Nathan's head dropped. In that moment he felt everything he worked towards being ripped away from him. After that things were just a blur. Nathan shifted uneasily on the couch and stared into the darkest corner of the room. *It's as if I asked her to swim. I asked her to swim and she just threw me in the deep end without any training, without any guidance. I'm drowning here,* he thought.

Twenty-four hours later, he was on a plane to Ireland. He received the call that evening to say his dad had died. The shame he felt as he remembered his first thought upon hearing the news gnawed at him; the shame that came with the relief that he could escape the situation, even if it was to attend his father's funeral. His eyes filled with tears and he felt a lurch in his chest.

The coffin was so small and he never got to say goodbye. *That is it for him,* Nathan kept thinking. No more worry, no more pain, nothing … just nothingness.

Nathan was ripped from his reverie when Fionn burst into the room.

'I just got a call; we've got to go.'

Startled, Nathan stood up immediately and wiped his eyes with the back of his hand.

'Grab whatever you need from the bag,' Fionn pointed to the yellow North Face bag next to the door. 'And a coat too. The boots should be alright for you. The weather's coming in, so prepare for the worst. I've got extras in the car.'

Nathan didn't get a chance to respond, Fionn was already gone. The front door slammed behind him.

The Wicklow Mountains

We always go back to what we know in times of stress.

With a press of the button on the steering wheel, Fionn disconnected the call to Hugo. Hugo was more than happy to stay in considering how the weather was changing. He was such a happy-go-lucky kind of guy, nothing ever seemed to get his back up.

'I'm sorry about tonight.' Fionn's eyes were focused on the road, and he was driving a little too quickly as they made their way through the backroads towards the Wicklow Mountains.

'That's alright. This is just another thing gone wrong this week,' Nathan said with a chuckle in a weak attempt to hide his disappointment. Fionn glanced to his left, quickly took in the look on Nathan's face and then returned his eyes to the road.

'Yeah, I'm sorry about your dad. These are always tough times. A few drinks would have been good — raise a toast to him.'

'Thanks, man,' said Nathan. There was silence between them then. Fionn waited patiently, he knew there was more. 'It's not just that though.' Nathan paused. 'Things are a bit shit at work too.'

Fionn glanced at him. Nathan was looking out of the passenger window into the growing darkness. 'What do you mean? Your new job? I thought it was the job of your dreams. Aren't you looking after a team of people now? Didn't you ace the interview.'

Nathan permitted himself a smile as he remembered how easily the answers had come to him during the interview. How he demonstrated a real understanding of empathy and shared examples of the things that had prepared him for this role. How he had confidently told them that he was the best candidate and that no one would work harder. He scoffed to himself.

'Yeah, but it's not working out the way I hoped it would. I've inherited a bunch of arseholes.' Nathan glanced over at Fionn again to judge his expression. His face was blank. His concentration on the road ahead was intense. They'd left the city roads behind and the road ahead narrowed and snaked into the countryside.

'You wouldn't believe it. The other day I was at my desk and there wasn't a sign of any of them. About forty minutes later they sauntered into the office laughing and joking. Apparently, they had all gone for a team coffee and they didn't bother to ask me. Clearly, they've got something against me. Maybe that's a good thing though? I mean a boss shouldn't get too close to his staff. There should be a clear line of hierarchy in case I need to have tough conversations, right?'

Fionn continued to listen while he concentrated on the road.

Nathan shifted in his seat and faced Fionn. 'And they never give me updates on how the project they're on is going. I have to go and search for the information and they give me the bare minimum. It's like pulling teeth.

I'm looking bad in management meetings because I don't have the latest information and can't talk comfortably about where things are at. It's really embarrassing. It's like they want me to fail.

'In the mornings they might be all chatting and having a bit of banter, but when I come in it all stops and they turn and look at their screens. They're out to get me. I'm at the end of my tether. In fact, just before I got the call about my dad I had a one on one with Claudia, my boss.' Nathan fell silent and turned back in his seat to look out of the side window.

Fionn took in the sullen look on Nathan's face that was reflected in the window. 'How did that go?' he asked gently.

A few seconds of silence passed between them.

'Not good,' was all Nathan could bring himself to say.

Nathan's feet were hot with the two pairs of socks and boots tied up past his ankles. It had been a long time since he'd been hillwalking, although he and Fionn used to head off most weekends and cover all the notable peaks around Ireland. Part of him looked forward to getting back out there, even if it was impromptu and he was wearing Fionn's gear. The car was heating up to an uncomfortable level; he shouldn't have put on the coat before getting in. Fionn was looking very comfortable. His heavy clothing was in the rear seat. *Clearly I've been away from this far too long.*

Nathan took a breath ready to launch into another tirade when Fionn's phone rang.

'Sorry, mate. I've got to take this.' He clicked a button on the steering wheel. 'Hey Sophie, I've got my mate, Nathan from New Zealand with me. We're about forty minutes out. What's the craic?'

'Kia ora, bro!' Sophie had an instantly likeable voice, but Nathan played down any friendly connection.

'Hey, Sophie, what's up?'

'It's all good, mate. All good in the hood,' she replied. Sophie turned her attention back to Fionn. 'So, I'm due to meet Aisling at the main car park in about five minutes; she's there already. The situation is that a fifty-four-year-old male was supposed to be home three hours ago. His daughter became concerned when he didn't answer his phone and called it in. Aisling found the car and his mobile is still plugged into the dashboard. He probably went off without it. Apparently he's new to hillwalking and his navigation skills are pretty average at best — her words, not mine.'

'Anna, Ciara and Sienna are on their way; they'll probably get there before Nathan and me. I've asked them to set up in the car park, just in case things turn to custard. As you are the first on the scene, how would you like to handle things?'

Nathan was quietly listening in, but at this comment he looked over at Fionn. He thought Fionn was clearly the laissez-faire leader. Hands-off and high trust. That stuff never works. How could Fionn be the lead coordinator of the mountain rescue team? Surely a more autocratic controlled style was required in this situation. You have to be clear about what you want everyone to do. You can't leave it up to them — it will be chaos.

Sophie was explaining that she and Aisling would take the longer route to the summit. It was the easier of the two main approaches to the summit and there was a better than average chance he would have taken this route. Besides, it was getting dark and they would need to take advantage of whatever light was available. Nathan noticed this for the first time. The car headlamps had automatically come on and illuminated the way forward.

'Sounds good. I'll likely grab Ciara and the three of us will take the other route.' Fionn paused. 'And Sophie ...' he added.

'Yeah.'

'Remember to bring your mobile phone.' The call ended with a chuckle from the other end.

They travelled in silence for a minute or two before Nathan spoke. 'Don't you think you should have taken greater command of the situation?'

Fionn looked at Nathan briefly. The question clearly interrupted his thoughts. 'Whaddaya mean, greater command?'

'Well, I thought you were the lead coordinator? Shouldn't you be giving the orders?' Fionn was quiet so Nathan continued. 'I mean, I always like to know what's going on, so I'm in control of things. You know, so if something goes wrong I can fix it. If everyone was making their own decisions it would be chaos. You can't run a team like that.'

Fionn was clearly put out by his friend's criticism but pushed down his irritation. 'Sophie's a good operator. We've been working together for a long time. She doesn't need to be told what to do, I trust her implicitly.'

Unconvinced, Nathan continued his argument. 'Yeah, but it was like she was telling you what she was going to do. What if you had a different idea? Wouldn't it only lead to an argument?'

'Don't get me wrong, Sophie and I have crossed swords over the years, but it's always been a respectful and professional conversation about the point of difference. I know she'll always have my back and I'll always have hers.' Fionn paused to let his viewpoint sink in. 'How's the autocratic leadership style working for you with your team?' he added.

Nathan squirmed in his seat. 'Good point,' he replied.

They drove in silence for a short while.

'There are more than the laissez-faire and autocratic leadership styles out there, you know,' Fionn said, not unkindly. Nathan didn't know, and he felt embarrassed at not knowing. He was the great leader after all.

Wasn't it him who nailed the interview with his knowledge about leadership?

'The autocratic style is certainly one of them and it has its place, but so has the laissez-faire approach. It's how you use them and the others that really matters. If you only use one of the styles it's only going to work on a limited number of people and only in a certain number of situations,' Fionn continued.

'I'm not sure I agree with you. All the leaders I've ever worked under have always been autocratic in nature and it prepared me well enough.'

'Is that true?'

Those three words, as simple as they were, halted Nathan in his tracks. He couldn't help re-evaluating. 'Well, not if my current situation is anything to go by.'

The light was fading more rapidly now. The clouds were becoming darker, angrier and nothing was visible beyond the arc of the car's headlamps.

'It's not your fault. I mean, if I was to ask you, how do we really learn to lead?' Fionn said.

'I guess it's from others. Watching them and acting the way they act in certain situations.'

'That's right — that's exactly right. We model leadership on those we've followed in the past. The books and seminars can be useful but only if you're aware of one salient point.'

When Fionn didn't offer the answer, Nathan turned to face him. 'Which is?'

'We always go back to what we know in times of stress.' Fionn paused to let this sink in before continuing. 'You said you nailed the interview. You were probably giving all the book answers. Is that not true?'

'Well, yeah. Of course. That's the way I'd like to be as a leader, but it's not as easy as you make it sound. There are real decisions that need to be made in tough timeframes too. I have to be seen to be in control. I'm a leader, right? I mean what's my job if I'm not not in control of things?' Nathan was becoming frustrated. 'The theory just doesn't work in real-life situations,' he blurted out.

'Real situations like mountain rescue,' Fionn said a little cheekily.

Nathan remained quiet. He calculated how much longer to the car park, but really he had no idea. *I hate being out of control,* he screamed in his own mind.

'Look, I'm not gettin' at you. It's just a different way of looking at things, I guess. I mean, of course, you're going to be a commanding type of leader if that's what you've been exposed to; it's only natural. It worked for you in those situations because you're the type of character who can suck it up and get on with things? Did it work for everyone in your old teams though?'

He has a point, Nathan thought reluctantly. All the teams he'd belonged to hadn't exactly been fun to be a part of. There was high turnover, high stress and a lot of finger-pointing and covering your own back.

'Being in a leadership role is always going to be stressful. That's why that point I made about always going back to what we know in times of stress is particularly important for leadership. If our default behaviour is to try and control people, this becomes even more exaggerated when we're experiencing stress.' Fionn paused. 'And people don't like to be controlled.' Fionn paused again for emphasis and when Nathan didn't say anything he carried on. 'Therefore, we need to train ourselves to respond instead of reacting. Keeping a lid on unhelpful stress responses can consume a lot of cognitive energy if we try to do it consciously. That's why we need to ensure it runs in the unconscious as much as possible. This allows more cognitive resources to be available for the other visible and equally important tasks of leadership — problem-solving and decision-making.'

This was starting to make more sense to Nathan. 'So how do you do that when your default style has always been autocratic or commanding?'

'It's useful to learn the theory from books and so on, but the real gold is in putting it into practice. Trying it out, making mistakes, regrouping and going again. Feedback from your peers and your team is really important here. Even indirect feedback.' Fionn didn't have to spell it out. All Nathan had been getting over the last couple of months was indirect feedback from the team.

'You see,' Fionn continued. 'We use a different part of our brain to learn leadership skills than to learn to code or to balance the books. The same is true for communication skills, emotional regulation, negotiation, and building relationships. Coding and accounting for example are learnt and stored in the neocortex part of the brain. Some people refer to it as the thinking brain.' Fionn paused and looked at Nathan before continuing. For Nathan's part he wasn't sure what psychology had to do with things, but it was interesting all the same.

'Go on,' Nathan said.

'The neocortex learns very quickly — it's what it was designed to do. Leadership skills are learnt and stored in the limbic system, the emotional part of the brain. This is important to know because the limbic system is a much slower learner than the neocortex. It's a much slower learner because it's not a case of learning something new, it's more a case of learning on top of already deeply ingrained habits. I mean we've been communicating since the day we were born, but if our communication style isn't working for us it makes sense to learn to communicate differently, right?' Fionn didn't wait for a response. 'The same is true for leadership. How the limbic system learns is through lots of practice and lots of repetition.' Fionn paused and glanced at Nathan who was deep in thought. 'Lots of practice and lots of repetition.'

There was still no reaction from Nathan, so Fionn jokingly offered his wisdom again. 'Lots of practice and lots of REP-ET-IT-ION.'

As his reverie was broken, Nathan laughed for the first time in what seemed like a very long time.

Nathan's curiosity had increased. 'You mentioned there were more than the autocratic and laissez-faire leadership styles. What are the others?'

'We'll have to chat later, we're here.' He swung the car off the road onto a gravel surface. The lights followed the arc of the wheels and illuminated three figures at the far end of the car park.

'Come on, I'll introduce you to the others. Kia ora, bro!' Fionn laughed. 'That's hilarious!' The door slammed behind him and left Nathan alone with his thoughts. He reached into his pocket and pulled out his phone, brought up the notes app and started capturing what he could remember of their conversation.

The Plan

The questions were building up in his mind and he was determined to find the answers.

Nathan tucked his phone back into his inner coat pocket and got out of the car. The cool air on his face was welcome after the oppressive heat. He made his way over to the others who were deep in discussion.

The mountain reared up behind them, a dark colossus standing defiantly against the oncoming storm. The wind rattled the map laid out in the boot of Anna's van; four hands spread to the corners to keep it from blowing into the abyss. Nathan noted that the van was packed to the brim with camping gear, water canisters and cooking utensils. Fionn looked up briefly.

'Everyone, this is Nathan. He's over from New Zealand and he'll be tagging along with me and Ciara tonight.'

All eyes turned to Nathan, who was temporarily blinded by the head torches that turned in his direction. They nodded in unison.

'Kia ora, everyone!' Nathan said a little too enthusiastically. No one acknowledged his attempt at Kiwiana except for Fionn who stifled a laugh before getting back to the matter at hand. He called Sophie and put her on speaker.

'Yellow!' came Sophie's up-beat tone.

'Great, can you bring Aisling in on this call? I want to set the scene.' There was static from the other end of the line before Sophie gave a one-word response. 'Go!'

'Okay folks, we've got a relatively inexperienced hiker somewhere on the mountain. It looks like he doesn't have a phone with him or any other way of reaching out for help. His daughter called earlier when he didn't come home. She was expecting him about three hours ago. That means he's probably under prepared for the incoming weather, he's tired, short of food, and may even be injured. It's unlikely the rescue chopper can come out in this weather, so as first responders it's on us. Our goal is to find him, assess his condition and bring him home safely with a story to tell his grandkids. Any questions?' Fionn looked around and made eye contact ever so briefly with the rest of the team. There were no questions. 'All good, Sophie and Aisling?'

'All good this end. We'll continue on our course and be in touch if we find anything,' said Sophie.

'Roger that,' Fionn said before he ended the call. He put his fist out in the middle of the group. Anna and Sienna fist bumped him and Nathan followed suit. Fionn was retracting his fist when Nathan awkwardly fist bumped the air. No one seemed to notice, but he could feel the redness in his cheeks.

'Okay, Anna, Sienna,' Fionn said as his voice picked up in energy and intensity. 'It's awesome you got here so quickly. I see that you've pretty much got everything we need well sorted in your van — it all looks so accessible too, which is awesome. Nice work.' Fionn paused to let his words sink in.

Anna nodded. She was mildly embarrassed.

'I need you to move the van to that side of the car park. To make sure the car tent is buffeted from the wind. It's going to be a wild one by the looks of things. We don't know the circumstances that Stephen, that's our guy, is in. He could be suffering from hypothermia by the time we get to him,' he added and glanced at Anna, careful not to blind her with his head torch.

Anna nodded.

'Sienna, make sure there's a sleeping bag set up with a thermal blanket ready to go. Do a quick check on the first-aid kit from Anna's van. Any other first-aid supplies can be found in the back of my car. We don't need an ambulance at this stage but be ready to put in the call if required.'

Sienna nodded.

'It's really great to have you both on the team. I know this is your first rescue, so far you're doing great.' After a brief pause to ensure his words were heard he turned his attention back to the map in front of them.

Nathan, watching quietly, smiled to himself. *So much for trusting your people,* he thought to himself. *That last interaction sounded pretty autocratic and commanding wrapped up with a nice bow.*

Nathan strained to look between Sienna and Ciara to see the map. Fionn shifted to the side. 'Okay, Ciara. You know the situation, what are your thoughts about how we should approach our ascent?'

Ciara moved a little closer and leant in towards the map. She traced her finger along a ridgeline. 'Right, Sophie and Aisling have taken this route here. It's the most common and straightforward way to the top. Stephen is reportedly new to hillwalking so it's very likely this is the direction he took. We haven't heard from them yet, so we can assume they haven't had any luck locating Stephen. I propose that we take this route here.' She drew another route with her finger. 'It's steeper and a little more challenging, but overall it's a shorter, more direct route.'

'Nice work,' said Fionn. 'Let me just check. What are the potential risks of taking this route. What are the pros and cons?'

Ciara thought for a moment. 'Well, the pros are it'll be a quicker way to the top and with the weather coming in we'll want to get up and back in as short a time as possible. Hmmm … however, with the weather coming in, this part here will be trickier and we'll be exposed to the winds.' Her finger jabbed at a particular area of the map where the concentric lines were closer and closer. 'We don't want to risk any of us getting injured, that would be a disaster.'

'Very good,' said Fionn. 'Great insights. So what do you think we should do instead?'

Ciara thought for longer and the area of the map she was concentrating on was illuminated more from her head torch as she leant into it. We should stay on this side of the ridge. This will protect us from the worst of the weather and it's also possible that Stephen, if he was on his way back down might have taken the same approach.'

'Nice,' that was all Fionn needed to say. Ciara refolded the map and everyone stepped back from the boot of the van. 'Let's get going.'

Nathan, consumed by his thoughts as he'd watched his unexpected mentor in action, was suddenly jarred into action. There was something about the route that Ciara suggested that didn't sit right with him; he couldn't quite put his finger on it, but he told himself that Fionn would've picked up something if anything was wrong. He ignored this lingering doubt and ran back to the car, grabbed his backpack and met Fionn and Ciara at the edge of the stream as they made their first steps into the darkness. Anna and Sienna were already repacking the van, getting ready to move it as per Fionn's suggestion … or order. Nathan hadn't quite figured out which.

The feeling of the soft turf under his feet flooded his mind with memories, and a sense of excitement and adventure gripped Nathan. He couldn't help smiling to himself. How many times had he and Fionn taken this very same route to the summit over the years? Even though the wind was blowing more strongly now and he could feel the temperature had dropped, he was quite warm under his, or Fionn's, layers. The familiar sound of gorse scraping against the gators set up a nice rhythm for his steps as he followed Fionn, who in turn, followed Ciara up the mountain.

After a couple of hundred metres, Fionn called out to Ciara. 'How are we doing with our navigation?'

Ciara looked towards the ridgeline and her eyes followed it to the mountain summit. 'Pretty good,' was her response.

'How do you know?' asked Fionn. Nathan strained to hear the words above the wind but felt another learning moment coming on, so he shuffled closer.

'I can see the outline of the ridge against the skyline.' Ciara continued to march forward with her head down to protect her face against the wind.

Fionn paused for a moment. He retrieved a map folded small enough to fit into his chest pocket but large enough to show the route they were on. He placed his compass on the map and twisted it to line up their direction. *Two degrees,* he said to himself. He turned to Nathan, gave a quick nod and proceeded to follow Ciara who was about twenty metres ahead.

Disappointed that no words of wisdom came his way, Nathan took a quick look in the direction of travel. Only Ciara's and Fionn's head torches were visible in the blackness. He sighed heavily before starting off again, taking his first step and then the next and then the next. Soon, the rhythm of his gaiters brushing through the gorse took over and his legs continued as if they had a mind of their own. They continued to walk in silence, but it wasn't long before the weather took a turn for the worse. Within moments, everything had changed, and not for the better. Low cloud started to blow in from the south west and with it came the rain. Nathan pulled his hood lower over his eyes and continued to trudge on. His legs were starting to burn at the relentless pace up the mountain slope and he sucked in air harder than he would have liked at this stage of the walk.

Once again Fionn called out to Ciara. 'How's our navigation?' Ciara stopped and looked up in the same manner as before. Even through the darkness and the low cloud, Nathan could see the panic on Ciara's face. 'I assume we're still heading in the right direction,' she said sheepishly.

'Okay, how would we know?' asked Fionn. He had a way of inquiring that was gentle and prevented a defensive reaction in Ciara.

'Map and compass?' Ciara replied.

'Spot on,' Fionn said. 'We should be checking our bearing every one hundred metres, that's about one hundred steps. I know it's a pain in the arse, but it would be a lot worse if we ended up over the edge of a cliff.'

As Fionn was talking, Ciara was lining up her map and compass. 'I can't get a bearing. There are no landmarks. I can't see anything with the cloud.' Ciara's shoulders dropped and she mouthed a few expletives as she looked up the mountain.

'That's alright, C. I've been tracking things. C'mere, I'll show you where I think we're at and you can take things from there.'

Ciara sidled up to Fionn, realigned her settings and took the lead again.

Nathan was left with his thoughts as the hypnotic rhythm of his footsteps took over. The last couple of hours had been interesting. He noticed that Fionn had different ways of delegating tasks. Initially, he thought he was very laissez-faire with Sophie, but he was much more direct when speaking with Anna and Sienna. Then he changed tack again with Ciara, firstly asking her thoughts about the route but gently challenging her if he thought Ciara might have been missing something or would take an action that would lead to an unnecessary risk. Now, even though he knew Ciara was making a mistake he let her continue on for a bit before pulling her up. Why didn't he tell her to use her map and compass when he first identified the issue? Surely that would save time? Maybe there was a little more to Fionn's leadership style than he gave him credit for. The questions were building up in his mind and he was determined to find the answers before getting on the plane back to New Zealand.

The First Lesson

Can you absolutely know that that's true?

A bird sounded in the distance, its cry carried to them on the wind. They continued their relentless pace. Ciara stopped briefly every one hundred metres, reset her direction and took off again. Every time they started up again Nathan could feel the pain in the side of his knee gradually getting worse. It was almost imperceptible in the beginning, but as they continued to march over the uneven terrain it became noticeably more painful. Thankfully, the terrain evened out and Nathan took a few extra quick steps to catch up with Fionn. He smiled at him. 'It's been a while since you've been in the hills. You enjoying it?' Fionn asked.

'Surprisingly enough I am,' Nathan said and laughed. 'It would be nice to see some of the scenery though.'

Nathan noticed that even though Fionn continued to walk in a direct line behind Ciara he was constantly looking from side to side as he went.

Although with the limited vision, Stephen could be lying dead five metres on either side of them and they'd never see him. At least the rain had eased off, thought Nathan.

'I have a question for you.' Nathan broke the silence.

'Shoot,' Fionn replied.

'I notice you're a bit flippy floppy when giving out tasks. Is it because you've got favourites or something?'

Fionn laughed. 'No, I wouldn't say I've got favourites. I mean, Sophie and I have known each other a long time, so I suppose I have a deeper relationship with her than with the others. Does that answer your question?'

'Well, no,' said Nathan. 'I guess what I wanted to know is why you're different when giving out instructions to everyone. I mean, with Anna and Sienna you were quite direct when you told them what you wanted them to do. With Ciara you've been pretty lax even though you knew she was making mistakes, and with Sophie, you just let her do whatever she wanted.'

'Crikey!' said Fionn. 'When you put it like that you make me sound like I'm all over the place.' He laughed again. 'There is a method to the madness though.' Fionn thought for a minute. 'Let me ask you a question … would you delegate tasks to someone who is very experienced in the same way you would to someone who is just starting out?'

'Of course not!' Nathan replied over enthusiastically, although deep down he recognised that this is exactly what he had been doing.

'That's right,' continued Fionn. 'If you delegate to someone who is new to the team or the craft in the same way you do to someone who is very experienced they won't have enough information to carry out the task. It's likely they'll get stressed out and fail. Their confidence will be knocked and they'll be reluctant to try anything new. By the same token, if you delegate a task to someone who is very experienced in the same way you would with someone just starting out it will come across as micromanagement. They'll get frustrated and leave.'

'I see, so that's why you gave Anna and Sienna such clear direction and set out your expectations the way you did. They're new to the team.'

'That's right,' said Fionn. 'Anna does a lot of hiking and camping herself, but that's only part of what we do. She's learning the ropes, as is Sienna.'

'But how do you get to the point where you can let people off to do their own thing and know that they'll do a good job?'

'Good question. There are a couple of factors to consider. Firstly, it's important that the person has the right capabilities to do the job, that's a no-brainer. But equally important is to ensure that the person has the right attitude to do the job. If both of these factors are present then trusting the person is made a lot easier.'

'Well, that's me screwed then, isn't it?' Nathan said.

'How do you mean?'

'Well, all my team hate me and their attitude sucks. They're reluctant to do anything I tell them. They just make life so much harder than it needs to be.'

'Is that true?' asked Fionn. Those three words again.

But this time it was true.

'Yes, it is absolutely true. They're all arseholes!'

'Can you absolutely know that that's true? That they're all arseholes and their attitude sucks? Can you know for sure, without doubt, that that's true?'

Nathan knew the answer. He, of course, couldn't know that it was absolutely true the way Fionn put it. A sense of frustration rose in him.

'Are you saying it's my fault?' Nathan blurted out more aggressively than he intended.

Fionn laughed again. 'No, not at all! I'm just holding up a verbal mirror for you. I'm guessing your answer is that you can't know that it's absolutely true. And that's right, we can never know the absolute truth about these things because they're all subjective. They may feel pretty concrete in nature, but the reality is it is just our thoughts that make them feel this way. Can I ask you another question?' Fionn paused, waiting for permission to continue.

Nathan nodded.

'How do you react when you think that thought? Who do you become? How do you treat others?'

'How do I react when I think they're all arseholes and their attitude sucks?' Nathan asked more to the wind than to Fionn.

Fionn nodded.

'I guess I get impatient and more aggressive with them when they make mistakes or don't give me the information I need when I need it.' Nathan's thoughts drifted back to a recent team retrospective. The team had completed a piece of work and it was time for a quick debrief. There was one particular issue that took far too long to resolve and it really became a bug bear for him. When it was brought up at the meeting the team dismissed it as a joke and "just one of those things". Nathan nearly lost his mind. He went on a tirade and accused the team of being incompetent and not being diligent enough about their work. Something like that should have been caught much sooner and if they had good coding practices it never would have happened in the first place. Everyone at the table went silent. No one moved, the coffees remained on the table; the muffins untouched. Nathan had to hold himself back from standing up and banging on the table to make the point. It wasn't until Claudia gave him a dressing down and literally told him to pull his head in that he stopped his onslaught of blame. For the rest of the meeting, Nathan sat there with a sullen look on his face. Claudia continued with the agenda, but the mood was set. People barely contributed and the joviality with which the meeting started was gone.

'I guess I become a bit of an arsehole myself. I'm kinda embarrassed to be honest.'

'I know this is tough. Let me ask you, who would you be without that thought?' asked Fionn gently.

'Who would I be without that thought?' repeated Nathan. 'I guess I'd be more patient and trusting of the team. I guess I'd let them get on with things and believe that they're probably doing their best. It is a high-pressured environment so mistakes are going to happen. If I didn't have that thought I'd probably be more supportive of them, guide them more when required, you know?'

Fionn did know. He reflected on his own journey into leadership and recognised his own pitfalls. 'So, are you ready for the last question?'

Nathan laughed nervously. 'Sure. Give it to me!'

'If you were to turn your original thought around; the thought "they're all arseholes and their attitude sucks" what would that sound like? And does it sound as true or truer than the original thought?'

'You mean, if I said, I'm an arsehole and my attitude sucks?'

'Yes, that's the idea,' said Fionn. 'I'm not saying that's true but does it feel as true or truer to you?'

'Yeah,' said Nathan. 'It probably feels truer to be honest. Jeez, I've been such a douchebag.'

'Don't be so hard on yourself. We've all been there. In fact, if we had the time I'd ask you to write down your thoughts before starting with the four questions.'

Nathan was puzzled. 'Why's that?' he asked.

'Writing down the thought freezes it in time. Our thoughts are so fleeting it's difficult to challenge them. When we have a negative thought we tend to spiral downwards and this leads to irrational and emotive thinking. Neither are very useful in a leadership position. That's what my coach tells me anyway.' Fionn laughed.

'You have a coach?' Nathan couldn't believe his ears.

'Of course! I've found it the quickest way to improve and grow. A coach tailors the conversation to your needs in the moment and they hold you to account. They catch you on your bullshit, so you can't help but improve. My coach has encouraged me to use that exercise any time I get caught up in negative thinking about myself, others or a situation. I've found it really useful.'

Nathan and Fionn were so caught up in their conversation that they nearly bumped into Ciara who had stopped to take a bearing.

'We're not going to have much luck out here tonight,' Ciara said to Fionn. Nathan held back, caught up in his own thoughts. Fionn was right, he was being the arsehole. As uncomfortable as the recognition was, it also felt freeing. It was as if he now knew what he needed to do. Firstly, stop being an arsehole. He couldn't control their attitudes, but he could control his own. Secondly, he thought he needed to apologise. As uncomfortable as that would be, he felt it was the right thing to do. Those were a nice bunch of questions though. He grabbed his phone, shook off his gloves and tapped the questions into his notes app.

The Art of Delegation

Firstly, imagine a four-square grid or a window with four panes of glass.

Nathan had just finished typing into his phone when Fionn turned to him. 'We're going to keep going for another couple of kilometres. If we don't see any trace of him we'll backtrack. Unless we get a lucky break we're not going to find him.'

Nathan simply nodded. Ciara and Fionn turned to face back up the mountain, and with what seemed like an extra effort, continued the thigh-burning slog through the gorse with their heads down, into the wind.

They continued their rhythmic march through the gorse. Nathan was thankful for the clothing and boots Fionn had on hand. Being out in this weather without the gear would be miserable. He couldn't help but wonder if the pain in his knee was caused by the slightly too-big boots. He tried to distract himself from the pain and his mind wandered back to his life in New Zealand. Being married with two daughters made him feel the pressure to provide for them, to give them a nice life. He was always driven to succeed, to be the best. This was much easier when he had been a solo player. His success and the rewards he received were the results of his own hard work. It was a whole new ball game now he was reliant on others for his success. His thoughts were interrupted by a yell.

'Ahhh shit!'

Ciara was ankle deep in a marsh and Fionn was bent over laughing. It suddenly occurred to Nathan that that was what had been bothering him back at the van when they were planning their route. Nathan had fallen foul to the same fate in the past — soggy socks and squelching boots were in Ciara's foreseeable future. Fionn reached over to pull Ciara out. After a lot of swearing, Ciara eventually calmed down and got out her map. She peered closely, and sure enough there were the little black vertical lines along a longer horizontal line that represented the marsh symbol on topographical maps.

That was a bit mean, Nathan thought. He was sure Fionn would have seen these markings earlier on, which would've saved Ciara an uncomfortable few hours.

Ciara reset her bearings and took them off to the left of the marsh. It would take about ten minutes to get around it, but the alternative wasn't a pleasant one. When Ciara took off, still swearing to herself, Nathan caught up with Fionn.

'You knew that was there, didn't you?' Nathan asked.

Fionn simply winked in response.

'Why didn't you tell her in advance?'

'Because it was an above the waterline mistake,' said Fionn.

'An above the waterline mistake? You mean literally!'

Fionn laughed. 'No, not literally. It's just a coincidence that water was involved in this one.' He laughed again before continuing. 'Earlier we were talking about delegation. This is all part of it.' Fionn paused to gather his thoughts. 'Let's go back to the start of our conversation about delegation and build on it.'

Nathan nodded and Fionn continued. 'Earlier we talked about how we can't delegate tasks in the same way to a new person as we would to a more experienced person and vice versa but still set them up for success. Let me share my thoughts on how we set up people for that success regardless of where they're starting from.

'Firstly, imagine a four-square grid or a window with four panes of glass. Now, if someone is brand new they're not going to know a lot and that's okay. We want to encourage learning, while at the same time, we want them to feel they are contributing in a meaningful way. In this instance we would give them smaller tasks to complete and be very clear about what we're asking them to do. For example, in an office environment, I might say something like:

- Nathan, I want you to complete sections A, B and E of the programme office report.
- You'll find it under the reports template section on the company wiki.
- In order to get the information for these sections you'll need to talk to Sienna, Anna and Aisling, for example.
- When you've done your first draft run it by Ciara for peer review.
- When it's completed with Ciara's comments send it to the epmo@xyz.com email address.

'I'd then ask them if they had any questions and take as much time to set them up with everything they need to succeed. I'd tell them they can come back to me at any time and also that I'd like to check-in (it's not a check-up, by the way). I'd never leave them more than three days without checking and I'd arrange a time with them in advance. I call this quadrant the **High Direction, Low Context** quadrant. What I mean by this is I don't spend a lot of time giving them the context behind what I'm asking them to do. I don't overload them with information that isn't immediately relevant to the task at this moment in time. Does that make sense at all?'

Nathan thought about this. 'It kinda sounds like micromanagement, even for me.'

Fionn laughed. 'It certainly can come across this way if you don't have a conversation up front about why you're giving them such clear direction. I draw the grid and explain how I'd like to get them to the fourth quadrant as quickly as possible, but I want them to learn quickly and get a couple of wins under their belts at the same time.'

'Okay, that makes sense,' Nathan said.

'So clearly, we don't want them to stay in that quadrant for very long so we move to the top right as soon as they exhibit any kind of competency. In this quadrant, referred to as **High Direction, High Context**, we continue to give them clear direction, but now we start to add more context, so they can begin to understand more about why we do the task and its importance. For example, we might say:

- Nathan, I want you to complete sections A, B and E of the programme office report. *It's our team's responsibility to complete these tasks for the project management office. The other sections of the report are completed by teams 1, 2, and 3.*

- You'll find it under the reports template section on the company wiki. *We store it there because that's where we store all company reports; that way they can be accessed by people working in the office and working from home.*

- In order to get the information for these sections you'll need to talk to Sienna, Anna and Aisling, for example. *The reason you talk to Sienna, Anna and Aisling is because they are responsible for the key projects that need to be reported at this time. They've completed the same report as you over the years to know exactly what's needed.*

- When you've done your first draft run it by Ciara for peer review. *Ciara peer reviews all the reports that go "up". She's had a lot of experience in this area and is trusted, not only by the team, but also by the executive team. She'll give you any pertinent feedback to make the report "pop". Peer review is something we always do as a team. It has nothing to do with your capability, it's a quality assurance activity and speaks to the professionalism of the team.*

- When it's completed with Ciara's comments send it to the epmo@xyz.com email address. *The report is then picked up by the programme office which is then summarised for the executive team to make investment decisions.*

'All that additional information might not be necessary in the beginning but you can see how it will help the person develop more knowledge about why we do the things that we do. It also helps them understand the wider workings of the organisation outside of the team.'

Nathan nodded. It was all making sense. 'You used that approach earlier with Anna and Sienna. You told them what you wanted them to do and you told them why. You added the context to help them understand.'

Fionn nodded. 'Yep, well spotted. It's something I do deliberately. I'm always checking-in to see where people's capabilities are so we can continue to help them grow at the right time and in the right way.'

'You also wrapped it up and tied it with a nice bow, I noticed.' Nathan laughed.

'That's right, I used the old feedback sandwich,' said Fionn.

Nathan thought for a moment. 'You mean the shit sandwich? I didn't even notice.'

It was Fionn's turn to laugh. 'Feedback and delegation go hand in hand; you need to be able to master both to be an effective leader.'

'But I always thought the feedback sandwich should be avoided.'

'Like everything, if it's overused it becomes predictable and loses its impact, but we'll talk more about that later. Let me continue with the delegation model. Actually,' Fionn caught himself. 'There is a really useful proactive feedback approach I like to use on the right hand side of the grid. I call it the 30% – 80% feedback model.'

Nathan repeated it. 'The 30% – 80% feedback model. You'll need to explain that because it doesn't add up.' Nathan laughed again. He was enjoying the conversation. It was a great distraction from his aching legs.

'Boom! Boom!' said Fionn with a mock moan to his tone. 'How it works is, if I'm asking someone to produce something for me that is either completely new to them or a bit of a stretch, I'll ask them to complete the task to about 30% and then come back to me. For example, I'll ask them to create an outline, put in the headers, sub headers, a few words to describe the content in each section, rough diagrams, if required, that sort of thing. It's really creating the scaffolding or bones of the document. I'd then give them feedback on what they've produced. The main question I want to answer for myself is, are they on the right track? Have they included everything that is necessary or are they going off on a tangent? I want to catch this early. That's the 30% feedback part.'

'That makes sense,' said Nathan repeating what he heard to himself to remember it so he could write notes when they stopped.

Fionn continued. 'I'd then ask them to go away and put some flesh on the bones. Bring it up to 80%, I'd say. This includes fleshing out each section with more detail. The diagrams and images, if there were any, would need to be accurate, but I'm less interested in any grammatical or spelling mistakes, page numbers, that kind of thing. When it's completed to 80%, I'd ask them to come back to me, then we can tweak it as appropriate, so when they complete their first draft it's practically there. That's a great conversation to have. There's nothing worse than someone going away with an idea and going off on a tangent and coming back a few weeks later with something that has been a complete waste of time. That's soul destroying for them and me. It's another way of setting them up for success.'

'That's a great idea!' said Nathan, without trying to contain enthusiasm for this master class in leadership from an unlikely source. He had no idea Fionn knew all this stuff.

'We'll talk more about feedback later, but let's get back to our delegation model. In quadrant two, we'd give them more time before checking-in, and the duration comes down to the risk profile of the task and the competence they've demonstrated to date. Quick question. What would happen if we continued to keep the person on the right-hand side of the model?'

'Well,' said Nathan. 'They'd stagnate and you'd have to continuously keep telling them what to do.'

'That's right,' said Fionn. 'Ultimately, we want to get people onto the left-hand side of the grid. This is where we give them more responsibility and autonomy.'

'Like you do with Sophie,' said Nathan.

'Correct, except we can't just give them complete autonomy without fully understanding their skillset and approach to problem-solving. If we give them something important to do without checking their understanding first, it might knock their confidence and they may psychologically move back a quadrant or two. This is where we have to set the scene. We're clear about the problem and the outcome we're after and we ask them what they think.'

'That's exactly what you did with Ciara. You asked her what route she'd take, but then you asked her loads of questions to help her explore her thinking.'

'Ha! Ha! Very good.' Fionn laughed. 'That's exactly the approach we take. If the person's thinking is aligned with your own then you're sweet; however, if there's a gap between your thinking and theirs, it's important to ask the questions that might uncover any potential risks that could derail the task. You have to remember though, their way of achieving a task might not be the way you'd do it, and you've got to be able to let go of insisting they do it your way. People have to bring their own creativity and skill to the task. How close do they have to be before you're comfortable with things? Eighty per cent, seventy per cent? It really depends on the gravity of the situation. What's the risk profile of the task?' Fionn paused to let this sink in. 'What are your thoughts so far?'

Nathan summed it up in his mind before putting his thoughts in words. 'So, you outline the problem and the outcome you're after in relation to the situation, then you ask them how they'd approach it. If their thinking is aligned to your own, that's great, off they go. However, if you sense there is a particular risk that could derail them, you would ask questions to explore this to help them problem-solve. Lastly, you have to let go of doing things your way; there are many ways to skin a cat, as they say.'

'Very good,' said Fionn.

'Wait a minute though,' Nathan jumped in before Fionn could move on to the last quadrant which he was keen to hear about. 'I know you knew we'd hit that marsh area. Why didn't you correct Ciara when she was mapping out the route?'

Fionn couldn't help letting out a roar of laughter. So loud Ciara turned around to see what she was missing. She paused, took out her map and compass, reset her direction, and, Nathan suspected, started counting her steps from one again.

'You mean the above the waterline mistake?' Fionn laughed again. 'Imagine we're in a boat. If I ask someone to carry out a task and they say, well we should do this, this and this and I'm thinking … hmmm, if we do that, that and that, it will cause a hole in the boat above the waterline. What should I do? Should I have the conversation before or after the fact?'

Nathan thought for a moment. 'If the hole is above the waterline it's no big deal, I guess. We can still continue to sail to our destination and repair the damage on the way.'

'Yeah. That's right. It's a great learning opportunity for the person. Sometimes people learn best by making mistakes. It's our job to ensure they don't sink the boat or their own confidence. If they make the mistake it's no big deal, but they may also pick up on the mistake themselves as they work through the task or project or whatever they're doing. Do you think Ciara will ever make this mistake again?'

Nathan chuckled to himself. 'No, I guess not. In fact, I've made the same mistake myself in the past, and even though it's been a long time, I knew there was something to keep an eye out for on this particular route.'

'But what if it's a below the waterline mistake?' asked Fionn.

'If it's a below the waterline mistake then we'd need to ensure that doesn't happen. We'd ask them questions to help them problem-solve and reduce or eradicate the risk. Such as, for example, ask them about the pros and cons of taking a particular route.' Nathan winked at Fionn. 'You also did it early on, on the hike. You noticed Ciara wasn't counting her steps nor paying proper attention to the route. I remember you stopping to check and then you said two degrees. That was how much we were veering off track.'

'That's right, I wanted to see if Ciara would pick it herself. I was keeping an eye on things and knew it would be a good learning experience for her. Again, hopefully she'll remember this for the future.'

'So let me guess,' said Nathan. 'We call this quadrant the **Low Direction, High Context** quadrant.'

'Right again. The last quadrant is relatively straightforward. This is where you have absolute trust in the person; they're as competent as you are yourself. They have the right skills and the right attitude to get the job done to the required standard, so you just give it to them. There is a risk here as well though.' Fionn paused to see if Nathan jumped in with the answer. When none came he continued. 'The risk is that most leaders spend a lot of time with those members of the team who need the most guidance and therefore take for granted those who are most experienced and can work autonomously. Even though we don't have to spend time with them around tasks it's still really important to spend time with them to continue to build and maintain your relationship. That way, if anything happens that knocks them, they know they can always come to you for help and support, or even just a friendly shoulder to lean on.'

Nathan nodded and reflected on the phone conversation Fionn had with Sophie earlier in the car. 'That's the **Low Direction, Low Context** quadrant,' said Nathan.

'Correct,' replied Fionn. 'But in order to ensure these conversations go well we have to understand the Six Leadership Styles first.'

'What about giving feedback? You said delegation and feedback go hand in hand.'

'They do, we'll get to that. I promise,' Fionn said with a chuckle. 'Oh!' he added. 'There's just one more thing about delegation. As you progress in your career there are going to be even more demands on your time. That's when delegation becomes really important, so let me share an exercise my coach gave me to help me get focused and delegate appropriately.'

Nathan nodded.

'Firstly, keep a record of everything you do for a week. That includes meetings, writing documents, peer reviewing, management meetings, one-on-ones, you get the idea. Then, at the end of the week, get a separate piece of paper and draw a line down the middle of it. On the left-hand side transfer all those things from your week that only you can do. Be brutal with this part of the exercise. Then on the right-hand side transfer everything else. Are you with me so far?'

Nathan nodded and visualised the exercise in his head as Fionn described the steps.

'Lastly, review those items on the right-hand side of the page and use the XDS formula.'

'The XDS formula,' repeated Nathan. 'I'm not sure I've heard of that one,' he said cheekily.

Fionn pushed him playfully before continuing.

'X stands for **Cut**. Again, be brutal here. Put an X next to anything that doesn't add any value. Maybe it's some task you got sucked into in the past, like attending a project board meeting and you're not the right person, or something like that.

'D stands for **Delegate**. Put a D next to those tasks that *could* be delegated. You don't necessarily have to delegate the task but you could. For example, the team might require a level of training before you can completely hand over the task, or they might be extremely busy at the moment and now's not the right time; however, you can create a plan around these tasks to eventually offload them.

'Lastly, S stands for **Systematise**. How can you systematise some of the repetitive tasks that consume time? You can't cut them because they're important but they distract you from what's really important. With the evolution of AI there are so many tools out there that can take away those repetitive tasks. For example, I use an AI calendar scheduler. I share this with people, they get access to my calendar and if they need to move the meeting it all gets handled in the background.

'So there you have it. This has been a lifesaver for me. Give it a go, you'll be surprised at how much time you can actually save.'

'That's it. Time to turn around,' said Ciara. They'd reached the maximum they were going to go. Nathan's thoughts turned to Stephen. He was somewhere out on the mountain, alone and highly likely injured. Fionn took out his phone. No missed calls. He removed the glove on his right hand and typed something on the keypad.

'I've told the others we're heading back. There is nothing from Sophie or Anna, so I'm assuming they haven't had much luck either. Let's take five minutes before heading down.'

Nathan, delighted at the opportunity, plonked himself on the sodden ground, took out his own phone and typed what he could remember of the conversation with Fionn. He promised himself he'd write these notes in full on the trip home.

The Visionary

I have a strategy.

The fog came through in patches. The full moon was visible from time to time as the dark clouds, ushered by the wind, passed by overhead.

Now that the rain had stopped, Nathan pulled back his hood and enjoyed the coolness on the back of his neck. The pace was easier now that they were heading downhill, but he was mindful of placing his feet carefully as he went. It is so much easier to twist an ankle going downhill on uneven terrain than it is going up. Besides, he thought, with a heavy pack on your back it's more likely you'll break the bloody thing instead of spraining it. Even though the climb up the mountain was tough, Nathan had to admit that he was really enjoying it. Perhaps being distracted by the conversation with Fionn helped, but he thought it was more than that. Even though they didn't have any luck finding Stephen, the poor bugger, he felt he was part of something important. Something beyond his own internal focus, his own problems. *I wonder,* he thought, *is that the solution to changing your mood?* Getting outside of yourself and contributing to something worthwhile? Perhaps it was the exercise? He knew he'd pay for it in his legs over the coming days; post-exercise muscle soreness is a bitch, but, he admitted to himself, it's worth it. Maybe it's both. He quickly pulled off his glove and took out his phone, and wrote:

The antidote to low mood is giving back and focusing on others and exercise.

He had put everything back when he had another thought that was worth capturing. After grabbing his phone he wrote again:

And talking to friends ... a problem shared is a problem halved.

'How are the legs holding up?' Fionn asked and Nathan looked up from his phone. Fionn was waiting for him to catch up.

'Not too bad. I know I'll feel it in the morning.'

Fionn laughed. 'Yeah, I wouldn't fancy a thirty-six-hour plane trip cramped in a small seat with sore legs. You're definitely going to feel it.'

Nathan thought for a moment. 'Yeah, but it will be worth it, I think. Thanks for taking me along tonight. I was in a shite mood, but I'm feeling pretty good at the moment.'

'I'm glad you're here. It's been too long between drinks.' He laughed.

'Tell me, you mentioned earlier about six leadership styles. I'm curious to know more about these and if they might be of use to me with the team.'

'Sure thing. I've found them useful beyond theory to build a high-performing team, and more than that, help me articulate my own personal leadership philosophy.'

Nathan was intrigued; if he was being honest, he didn't have a clue how to really build a high-performing team or even where to start with a leadership philosophy.

'So there are six leadership styles and these come in order of their most positive impact on an environment: Visionary, Coaching, Affiliative, Democratic, Pace-Setter, and Commanding.'

Nathan repeated these to himself so he'd remember them later on. 'Okay, to be honest, the only one I've heard of in this list is Commanding … and I think I've got that one nailed.' He couldn't help laughing at himself, which was a nice change.

Fionn smiled. 'The best way I've learnt to remember and apply these is to think of them as they relate to four questions:

1. How does this leadership style positively impact the environment?
2. When would you use it?
3. What are the attributes or characteristics of this leadership style?
4. What other useful information is there around this style; especially, when can it all go horribly wrong?'

'When can it all go horribly wrong? What do you mean?' Nathan said.

'Well, even the Visionary style, the most positively impactful of them all, can have negative effects if used at the wrong time and in the wrong way. And even though the Commanding style is at the bottom of the list, it is certainly useful at the right times and when delivered in the right way; however, if Commanding or Pace-Setting are your default styles and these are the ones you use most often, it will destroy the morale of any team.'

'I see, so where do we start?'

'Let's start at the top. When you think of the Visionary style, what do you think is its impact on the environment and why?'

Nathan thought for a while. He was embarrassed that the answers didn't spring forth. Wasn't he the leadership guru after all? The hypnotic swish of his gaiters against the gorse filled his consciousness when he suddenly heard a different voice in his head. *It's okay to learn this stuff; give yourself a break.* He nodded to himself and miraculously his mind cleared enough for him to think more clearly about the question.

'The Visionary style is the most positively impactful leadership style because it gives people direction and clarity about where they're going,' he said. 'In my own experience, I've always found this somewhat motivating; it feels like you're a part of something important, something bigger than yourself.'

'That's right,' said Fionn. 'That's exactly what it does.'

'Don't underestimate the power of clarity. When people have no clear direction or are immersed in uncertainty it can lead to uncomfortable feelings such as anxiety, doubt, and fear, just to name a few. When a leader, someone they trust, puts their hand up and says, This is the direction we're going and this is why, people will get behind her, especially if it's well articulated and ... here's an important point ... AND it aligns with their own unspoken vision.

'Think about your own experience when an organisation is going through a change and the leaders don't, or in some cases, can't share the direction. People freak out. Now think about the power of being able to articulate a vision in a way that people can understand. Think about Martin Luther King's famous speech, "I have a strategy".'

'Wait! What! It's I have a dream, isn't it?' Nathan asked.

Fionn laughed. 'Of course it is. No one would get excited about an *I have a strategy speech*. It's, *I have a dream* because dreams speak to our emotions; they speak to the very heart of who we are. It's not an intellectual understanding, it's an emotional understanding and that's what moves people.' Fionn paused before deepening his voice …

I have a dream that one day every valley shall be engulfed, every hill shall be exalted and every mountain shall be made low, the rough places will be made plains and the crooked places will be made straight and the glory of the Lord shall be revealed and all flesh shall see it together. This is our hope.

'The language he uses is so poetic it can't help but capture people's hearts. But why is it that hundreds of thousands of people from all over America travelled thousands of miles to be there in that exact spot at that exact moment? If you think about it, back then very few houses even had a phone and if you think Dublin transport is bad, you can only imagine what it was like back then.' Fionn couldn't help chuckle at his own joke before continuing. 'Why is it that so many people made the arduous journey to hear King speak on that auspicious day?'

Nathan thought deeply about the question and after a while, Fionn, caught up in his own enthusiasm, told him the answer.

'It's because King was able to articulate what they were all already feeling. King was able to put into words what they already believed deep in their souls. Now, if you can do that with your team …' Fionn let that thought hang in the air before continuing. 'If you can help align your team's own personal vision with that of the organisation or your team, they will show up early and stay late because it's no longer work for them, it's something that they are aligned to. I often think that people fail at their goals because they have to push to achieve them; however, if those goals are aligned to a vision then people can't help but achieve their goals because they are pulled towards them.'

Fionn and Nathan walked in silence. Nathan was deep in thought. *What is my personal vision?* he asked himself. *What is the vision of my team?* He had no clue and didn't know where to start. He remembered Fionn said something about using the leadership styles to help create a personal leadership philosophy. That would be a good start. Excited to know more he turned to Fionn. 'So when would you use the Visionary style and when wouldn't you?'

Fionn seemed distracted. He was concentrating hard on his map and compass. Nathan hadn't noticed, but the fog had become denser again, and the wind had picked up. This was making navigation more difficult. Fionn looked up from the map and cursed to himself.

Ciara had stopped up ahead. She was staring intently at her map and compass and Nathan got the feeling that something was awry. Fionn tucked his map back into his pocket before they reached Ciara. Nathan also closed the gap.

'What's up?' he heard Fionn say to Ciara over the bellowing of the wind.

'I, er ...' Ciara paused, twisted her map around and turned her head. 'I think I've taken us off route.'

'How do you know?' asked Fionn.

'Well, the terrain we should be on should be steeper than it is now. The terrain under foot doesn't match what I think it should be under foot.'

Ciara pointed to where she thought we were on the map with an ungloved finger.

'I think you're right and I'm sorry, I was distracted and not paying proper attention,' said Fionn. Ciara looked at him with a confused expression on her face. Nathan was also confused. Ciara was the front person after all; it was her responsibility to navigate the route.

'Okay,' said Fionn. 'So define the problem.'

Ciara didn't need to think about it too much. 'We're not where we should be. It's dark and the fog is thick. There's a risk we could walk off the edge of a cliff or end up miles away from our planned end point.'

'Agreed,' said Fionn. 'So that sums up the current situation we're in. Now, considering that, what would be a good outcome?'

Ciara thought before answering. 'Having a good indication of where we actually are on the mountain, so we can continue with confidence.'

'Nice, that's what I was thinking too. So what can we do?'

'Well, I already tried to get a bearing of where we are, but it would only be guess work.'

'Okay, what else can we do?'

'We could wait until there's a gap in the fog and try to spot a landmark against the backdrop of the sky,' said Ciara.

Nathan had to hold himself back from blurting out, That's a ridiculous idea. You've got us lost. You need to come up with something better than that.

'Okay,' said Fionn. 'What else?'

Nathan was stunned by Fionn's patient demeanour. How could he not say anything in response to such a ridiculous suggestion?

Ciara thought for a moment. 'We could backtrack until the terrain feels like it's lining back up to where we think we are.'

'Okay. What else?' Fionn replied.

The energy in Ciara's voice picked up. 'I could use the GPS position on my phone and align it with the map. We could set a new course from there.'

'Cool,' said Fionn. 'So we've got three options, which one do you think is the best approach?'

'I like the GPS option.'

'Great, let's go with that one,' said Fionn as he patted Ciara encouragingly on the shoulder. Then he looked over at Nathan who was staring in disbelief. He simply smiled and winked. 'We'll be back on track in no time at all.'

Fionn and Ciara huddled in close. Ciara read out the coordinates on her phone and Fionn used the reference numbers on the edges of the map to line up the coordinates. He struggled to hold the map in the wind, so Nathan held onto the edges. The beams from three head torches bounced around the surface of the map. After a moment Fionn pointed to their location.

'There,' he said triumphantly. 'That looks about right and feels about right taking into account the decline underfoot too.'

Ciara nodded in agreement and she and Fionn conferred about a new route. Ciara's finger snaked down the map.

'Nice work,' he said. 'Lead the way.'

Ciara refolded her map, put her gloves back on and strode off confidently in the new direction. Nathan could see Ciara mouthing the words as she counted her steps. He knew she wasn't going to make the same mistake. After a few steps they resumed their walking formation with Ciara a few steps in the lead, Nathan and Fionn a little behind and walking as a pair.

'That was pretty impressive,' said Nathan when they were out of Ciara's earshot.

'What was?' asked Fionn.

'How did you hold yourself back from giving Ciara a tongue lashing? She clearly messed up and the consequences could've been quite serious. And it was you who apologised to her. What's that about?'

Fionn laughed at Nathan's disbelief about what he had witnessed. 'Ciara is doing a fantastic job. It's pretty difficult to navigate under the current circumstances. She's still learning. What good would it do to tear her apart? Think about it? A mistake was made, what should we, as a team, focus on?'

'Fixing the mistake, I guess. But …'

Fionn cut him off playfully. 'But nothing, gringo! Pointing the finger never helps. In fact, it shuts down creativity and problem-solving and we'll end up in a worse situation. We'd still be lost and Ciara would be pissed off. She already knows she made a mistake; I don't need to reinforce that. My job is to guide her out of it.'

'Okay, but why did you apologise? She was the one who messed up.'

'Although Ciara is responsible for navigating the route, who is accountable for the team?'

'You are.'

'That's right. So, I also have a responsibility for keeping an eye on things. I was enjoying our conversation so much I got distracted. Whenever something goes wrong in the team, as the leader, it's important to look in the mirror. Of course, when things go well, as the leader, it's important to look out of the window; i.e. give the team the credit they deserve. I'm not talking about taking the blame for every little thing, but taking an honest look at what I could have done differently is a healthy exercise. Don't be slow to apologise when it's warranted, mate.'

Nathan was left speechless. He wasn't sure his ego would allow him to apologise to his team even if he was in the wrong.

Fionn nudged Nathan's arm with his elbow. 'We need to close the gap with Ciara, the fog is thickening.' With that Fionn picked up his pace and jogged after Ciara. Nathan followed suit and the extra motion reminded him of the pain in his shoulders from the weight of the backpack. He pushed it to the back of his mind and caught up with Fionn.

'Sorry,' said Fionn as Nathan caught up with him. 'What were you asking before about the Visionary leadership style?'

Nathan was caught off-guard with the question and had to roll back his thoughts. 'Oh yeah, I was just asking when you'd use the Visionary style and when you wouldn't.'

'That's right. Quite simply, you'd use the Visionary style when the team or the organisation is rudderless. There's no clear direction. Yeah, people are coming into work, but if you ask them why, they don't really have an answer, or if they do it's likely to be more task related than anything else. You know, I do the accounts or I write code for such and such a system, but they don't fully understand the impact or contribution their actions are having. A vision is an extremely powerful intrinsic motivator. Helping people get clear on the why behind their actions is important work for any leader.'

'Got it,' said Nathan, fully convinced of the need to do this for his team. He was already thinking how it could start to make a difference. 'When wouldn't you use it?'

'You'd never not use it, I guess,' said Fionn thoughtfully. 'It can be used in the wrong way though. For example, what if a new manager came in and within a couple of weeks told the team they were heading in a new direction. What message do you think that would send to the team?'

'Well, I suppose it would give the impression that everything they'd been doing for the last however many years was wrong and he knew better.'

'That's right. It would suck. The team would likely push back, at least quietly, and think the new manager was out of touch. How could they make that assertion without fully understanding all the hard work that the team had put in over the months and years? How could they make that assertion without fully understanding how the systems and processes work? Not only is it disrespectful to the team, it's the height of ignorance and arrogance. You should never tear down a fence without understanding why it was erected in the first place.' Fionn was on a roll now. 'I remember I was leading a couple of teams in an organisation once and a new general manager came in and within two weeks she announced, "We're going agile ... whether you like it or not".' Fionn paused.

Nathan chuckled at the irony. 'Isn't agile supposed to encourage open communication and collaboration?'

'Yes,' replied Fionn, a little too loudly. Clearly this experience had left a lasting impression on him. 'Not only that but she went on to say, "In six months all the contractors will be gone and the relevant roles will be replaced by permanent staff". You can imagine what happened next. None of the contractors waited around for the six month deadline, they all picked up and left. They found new contracts elsewhere. Not only that, but the permanent staff didn't like that their friends were being treated this way and also looked for opportunities elsewhere. Within six months, fifty per cent of the department had left. Can you imagine the amount of intellectual property that walked out of the door during that period?' It was a rhetorical question. 'I'll never forget the last town hall meeting I attended. She was rabbiting on about the plans for the future and completely ignored the fact that people were overworked and the department was creaking at the seams. She finished up by saying, "So, is everyone clear on my strategy ... the strategy ... our strategy?" I couldn't help but break into laughter as I walked out of the room and submitted my notice.'

'She sounded like a piece of work.'

'Oh, she was. But, there are occasions when there isn't the time to fully understand the legacy systems or processes, or even to get to know the people as much as you'd like before setting a new direction. For example, if the organisation or the team is about to fall off a cliff, then tough calls need to be made, and need to be made fast. Having said that though, more communication, not less, about the reasons behind the change are necessary. Even if there is going to be collateral damage people have to understand the context, they have to fully understand the reasons behind the decision.

'Michael Watkins, in his book, *The First 90 Days,* outlines it very well. He talks about how, when you first take over a team or organisation, you need to take a close look at the business situation which can fall into four categories; Startup, Turnaround, Realignment or Revitalise, and Sustainable Success. He calls it the STaRS model which is useful for remembering it. The Startup and Turnaround phases very much fall into the *doing* category. These equate to the cliff analogy I used earlier. There simply isn't time to learn about the ins and outs of the organisation, action is what's required. However, if the team falls into either Realignment or Sustainable Success then there is likely to be more time for learning. I know I've only given you a brief overview but this is an important model and it is essential in helping you determine the right strategy for your team.'

Nathan wished he could stop and take notes and repeated to himself the salient points to jot down later. *STaRS model. Startup, Turnaround, Realignment, and Sustainable Success.*

'There's also one other thing you might need to consider. If the leader is working with a team of experts or even peers who are more experienced than she is, she could be viewed as someone who is misaligned or as someone with a grandiose vision. This can also cause cynicism within the team, which can lead to poor performance. The leader may come across as overbearing and undermine the spirit of the team as a whole.' Fionn looked at Nathan who was nodding his head pensively. 'So, to sum it up, if you can, take your time to get to know the team before introducing change.'

The wind continued to bellow in Nathan's ears and he noticed the terrain was becoming steeper with every step. The fog continued to drift by, thick in some patches and light in others. His legs were tired, especially his quads and the pain in his shoulders from the weight of the pack was becoming a constant. No amount of shifting the backpack around eased the discomfort.

'What about the attributes for the Visionary leader?' he asked Fionn.

'Well, based on what we talked about, why don't you tell me?'

Nathan thought for a moment. 'Okay … we talked about the need to be articulate so they can share the vision. They have to have empathy to understand the needs of the team; they probably really excel when change is necessary, so I'd say they need to be a change-agent, they need to be open and honest and transparent with their vision, their goals. Lastly, I guess the Visionary leader would have to have a lot of self-confidence to set a new direction especially if it's a change to the status quo.'

'Nice,' said Fionn. 'I think you've summed up the attributes very well. I like how you mentioned confidence and I think you're right. If you think back to the Covid19 pandemic, one thing the New Zealand Government did better than any other country in the world was set a different vision. Do you remember what it was?'

Nathan thought for a moment. 'You mean the vision of, *As a team of five million we will eradicate this virus from our shores?*'

'Yep, that's the one. I remember chatting with you at the time of the lockdowns and how successful they were in New Zealand. You lived it, you remember.'

'Yeah,' said Nathan. 'And the government put out guidelines too — *Stay safe, Stay home, Be kind.* It really worked. Within a few weeks there were no signs of the virus within the community and we could largely come and go as we pleased, wearing masks, of course.'

'That's right,' said Fionn. 'So think about it, in a short statement, *As a team of five million we will eradicate this virus from our shores,* everyone got it. That's a powerful vision. In a few short words everyone understood the need for the lockdown, everyone understood the need for wearing a mask, everyone understood the need to social distance. That's what a vision can do. In a few short words it impacts on people's decisions and people's actions. Pretty powerful stuff, huh?'

Nathan never thought of it like that but he remembered those weeks and months during the pandemic and the whole thing just seemed so easy. 'Yeah, I guess it is.'

'And the way the New Zealand Government wrapped those other statements, those values, around the vision was a stroke of genius. They provided more guidance to people about what they needed to do to get through.'

'Yeah, you couldn't go anywhere without being blasted by those messages. *Stay safe, Stay home, Be kind.* I mean, I still remember them a couple of years later.'

'That's right! Another thing your government did so well and something that's important to remember about a vision and about values.'

'What's that?' Nathan was lost.

'Well, how many bits of information are we bombarded with on a daily basis? Emails, texts, instant messages, direct messages, social media, news, radio, conversations. We are literally bombarded with information every minute of every day. Important messages get diluted so *if* we want a message to stick it's vital that we take every opportunity to express that message in different ways, so that even a couple of years later, it's still remembered.'

'Wow … that's awesome! I never knew there was so much to setting a vision.'

Nathan's head was bursting with information. *This is pure gold,* he thought to himself.

'The last thing to remember about the Visionary leaders is that not only do they guide the team toward a vision, they also help set the standards — think values — and hold people to account for their actions and their decisions.'

Ahead of them Ciara had stopped. She was taking off her backpack. 'I need a break. Can we stop for a few minutes?' she shouted above the wind.

'Sure thing,' Fionn replied. 'We've been making really good time.'

Nathan and Fionn walked up to Ciara, dropped their backpacks and sat down gratefully on them. All three were tired, and as Fionn and Ciara chatted about the planned route ahead, Nathan took out his phone and made a few notes.

The Coach

Theory never lasts beyond its first engagement with reality.

I've a quick question,' said Nathan. They were on the move again after taking a few minutes to rest and grab a snack. Fionn had packed a few nut bars. Ciara had her own, but Nathan was thankful; he didn't realise how hungry he was until he took his first bite.

'What's that,' asked Fionn. Ciara was a few paces ahead as per usual, she had the map in her hand and Nathan imagined her lips moving as she counted her steps to herself.

'If we were able to locate ourselves using GPS, why do we need a map and compass? Why don't we just rely on the GPS on our phones?'

'Good question.' Fionn laughed to himself. 'I'll let you figure that one out.'

Nathan thought it through but the answer didn't become clear.

'What if you lose your phone, or the battery runs out or there is some other problem related to the technology,' said Fionn.

'Okay, I got it,' Nathan said sheepishly. 'Tell me about the Coaching leadership style.' Nathan repeated the questions in relation to the Visionary style:

1. 'How does this leadership style positively impact the environment?
2. When would you use it?
3. What are the attributes or characteristics of this leadership style?
4. What other useful information is there around this style; especially, when it can all go horribly wrong?'

'Well, the Coaching leadership style is the second most positively impactful of all the styles but shockingly is the least used. It doesn't necessarily focus directly on the bottom line, but it does add to it indirectly because it builds a deeper sense of trust and loyalty. It enhances an individual's self-confidence by building on their essential skills and encouraging autonomy.'

'Woohaaa! Hold up. There's a lot in there already,' interrupted Nathan. 'I mean if it's impactful on the environment why is it the least used?'

'Why do you think?' replied Fionn. 'How often do you take the time to coach your team?'

'Well, never. I didn't know it was a thing. I wouldn't know where to start, and besides I simply wouldn't have the time to coach anyone. It's so much more effective to tell people the answer, isn't it?'

Fionn was smiling smugly.

'Isn't it?' asked Nathan meekly.

Fionn continued smiling. Nathan clearly had his answer but still couldn't reconcile spending time coaching a person when it was so much easier to tell them what they need to know in order to get back to work.

'Think back to the delegation model we talked about earlier. What would happen if we kept giving them direction?'

'Well, they'd continue to remain on the right side of the quadrant and never learn to think for themselves …' Nathan's words trailed off. 'Okay, I get it. We want them to start thinking for themselves, so they don't have to keep coming back to you for help. They'll learn to think through challenges and find solutions for themselves.'

'Very good. It's worth spending the time up front helping them grow their skills and knowledge and confidence in themselves so they become more autonomous and can add even more value. It's a valuable investment.'

'Okay, but who has the time to coach everyone on their team?'

'I know, I know,' Fionn said, his tone dripping with humour. 'I mean you're too busy doing all these things to work with your team to learn to do those things. Here's the thing, and this is important, we always find the time to do those things that are important to us. If you make coaching a priority you'll find the time and you'll start to see the benefits of that investment. It won't be immediate, but it will come.'

'Hmmm …' Nathan considered his leadership style and it couldn't be further away from the coaching style. He was very task focused, he never really had the time to focus on his team's development.

'I really wouldn't know where to start with this, if I'm being honest.'

'I'm glad you're being honest,' Fionn said, taking the piss. 'Only joking, you're not alone, and in reality it's not that hard. Firstly though, let's talk about the attributes of a Coaching leader. What do you think they might be?'

Nathan thought for a minute or two. 'They'd have to be a good listener for a start. They'd have to know a lot to be able to solve people's problems and people would have to trust them.'

'Nice ... two outta three ain't bad.'

'Oh?' said Nathan. 'Which one did I get wrong?'

'You're absolutely right when you say they have to be a good listener and they definitely have to be able to build rapport with people, and build that trust quickly, otherwise people might not open up, right?'

'Yep,' said Nathan. 'So are you saying they don't need to know a lot of stuff?'

'Not necessarily. The best coaches I know are very knowledgeable in many different areas. They have to be because people are complex and can have challenges in many areas of life. You said they'd need to know a lot to solve people's problems.'

'Well, yeah. Don't they?'

'It's not a coach's job to solve someone's problems. It's a coach's job to help the person find the answer for themselves. It's useful to have a wide knowledge base so you can ask the right questions and understand the terminology a person is using as they describe their problem. In reality, a good coach doesn't need to be an expert in the person's area. A coach's expertise lies in asking the right questions to help the person arrive at a solution that works for them in the context in which they find themselves.'

'I see,' said Nathan pensively.

'So to build on the traits of rapport and listening, other traits that are useful are emotional self-awareness, empathy, and, of course, the ability to ask questions.'

Nathan made a mental note: rapport, listening, emotional self-awareness, empathy and questions.

'What do you mean by emotional self-awareness?' asked Nathan.

'Awareness is hugely important to a coach. You see, you can't not communicate. We're always communicating something whether we're aware of it or not. Even when you're not saying something and holding back your frustration when someone says or does something stupid.' Fionn smiled and looked at Nathan out of the corner of his eye.

'Oh,' said Nathan sheepishly. 'You saw that, eh?'

Fionn laughed. 'That's just a simple example. We can never pass judgement on what a person does or says because it breaks rapport and if we break rapport, we lose trust. We lose trust and our ability to help the other person is lost.

'Emotional self-awareness is more than that though,' Fionn continued. 'It has to do with being aware of our own biases and unconscious needs too. For example, our need to be liked or our need to always have the answer, our need to please others or a fear of challenging another person in case it leads to conflict. A coach must learn how to challenge when appropriate, to use humour … *when appropriate,*' Fionn stressed the last couple of words.

Nathan laughed uproariously. 'Okay! Okay!'

'I get it,' Nathan continued after a pause. 'It sounds like a coach has to be quite flexible in how they communicate to maintain the levels of trust while helping the person reach a solution, even if it's a challenging conversation.'

'That's it,' said Fionn. 'How I like to define coaching is: Coaching is conversation … a conversation with a purpose.'

'I like that,' said Nathan. 'That's a very apt definition.'

Ciara had paused, map in hand, head down as she confirmed their path. Nathan and Fionn waited patiently in silence. Without a word Ciara turned her head, nodded with a smile and headed off again.

'Coaching seems like a really valuable tool. I can't see how it can go wrong. You mentioned earlier that all the styles, if used in the wrong way can have negative effects. How can coaching go wrong?'

'You'd be surprised. Some people don't want to be coached. Those who are very task focussed sometimes just want the answer so they can get on with what they're doing. This group need to be in the right mindset to reflect. The other thing to note is that, if we don't have permission to coach someone, it might seem as if we're getting too close, asking too many questions that aren't welcome.'

'Surely your coach doesn't ask for permission every time you have a coaching session.'

Fionn laughed. 'Of course not, but there's an explicit agreement in that context. I'm there to receive coaching. In a manager-employee relationship, unless it's explicit that the relationship will include coaching as part of their professional development, it's important to ask for permission.'

'How would you do that? I imagine asking if the person wants to be coached on a problem might cause them to retreat. Maybe I'm just thinking about myself and how I'd react.' Nathan was aware of his cheeks flushing even against the cold wind as he reminded himself of his own insecurities.

'No, you're right. Sometimes people just want to talk things through and sometimes they want to vent. How I go about it is to ask, 'Would you like to work through that together?' or 'Would you like to use me as a sounding board?' or, one of my favourites, 'Would you like to kick the tyres on that together?' Most of the time people are open to that and then I have permission to ask questions. You don't want to come across as too micromanaging; you know, getting into their business when it's not welcome.'

'Hmmm… as simple as that, eh?'

Fionn laughed again. 'Yes, as simple as that.'

'So how do you do it?' asked Nathan. 'You said one of the things that stopped leaders from coaching was knowing how to do it?'

'It's actually not all that difficult. With a bit of practice the conversation comes together really nicely. The approach I like to take is to follow the G.R.O.W. model.'

'The G.R.O.W. model? I've heard of that. In fact, I even went on a course about it. It wasn't that great to be honest.'

'Yeah, I've heard that before. Largely it comes down to how it's taught and how to use it in a more practical way. Theory is one thing, but theory never lasts beyond its first engagement with reality. Let's break it down. What do you remember from the G.R.O.W. model? What do each of the letters stand for?'

'Oh no … now I'm feeling the pressure,' Nathan said and laughed. 'Let me see. G stands for Goal. R stands for …' Nathan wracked his brains. 'I can't remember what R stands for, but O stands for Opportunities and W stands for Way Forward.'

'Not bad, not bad,' said Fionn as he nodded his approval. 'G stands for Goal, R stands for Reality, O for options or obstacles, and W stands for Way Forward. Well done. So the G.R.O.W. model goes in a circular direction from G to R to O and to W.'

Nathan remembered what this diagram looked like from his course and made a mental image of it.

$$
\mathbf{G}
$$

GOAL

W

WAY FORWARD

R

REALITY

O

OPTIONS/
OBSTACLES

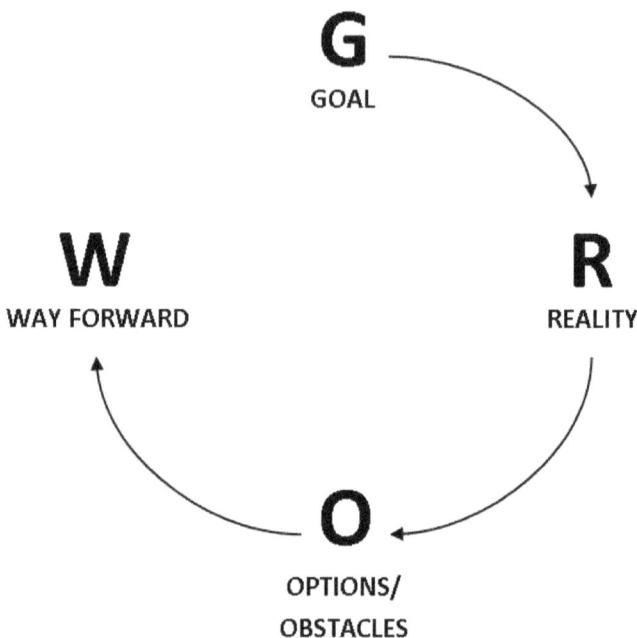

Fionn continued his explanation. 'The way the G.R.O.W. model is usually taught is to help the person identify their Goal, then their Reality, think problem or why they're stuck. Once we understand those things we ask the person to provide Options, enquire about potential Obstacles, if relevant before finally asking about the Way Forward or next steps.'

Nathan nodded, his memory from the workshop was coming back to him.

'The problem with that is most of the time people don't come to you with their goals in mind. They come to you with their problems. So really the model should be the R.G.O.W. model, but that doesn't sound as cool.' Fionn chuckled at his own joke.

'So, what do you mean by Reality?' asked Nathan. 'Is that the problem definition?'

'That's exactly what it is. The Reality step is exploring their reality of the situation, their problem. The reason it's called Reality is because reality is subjective. The only reason a person gets stuck is because they believe they are out of options. They believe that in that moment their reality, their perception of the world, is the reality.'

Nathan looked confused so Fionn went on. 'Have you ever had the experience of someone coming to you with a problem and you can see the solution straightaway, but for some reason, the other person is completely blind to it?'

'Yeah, of course.'

'That's what I mean by reality being subjective; they can't see it, but you can. You've got a different reality to them and therefore aren't unnecessarily stuck. That's what coaching does, it helps expand the person's model of reality ... their model of the world.'

It had never dawned on Nathan before why coaching is so powerful. It can literally change someone's life by giving them a new perspective on things.

'Okay, I get it. So when would you use this model?'

'It's best to use it when the person is stuck with a problem you believe they hold the answer to, even if they can't see it yet. For example, when Ciara got stuck earlier.'

'Oh my God!' said Nathan. 'You used the model on Ciara to help her come up with the solution to her problem — she was literally lost!'

'That's right,' said Fionn. 'And it didn't take that long either. This is true for most coaching conversations you're likely to hold with your team. They have the answer, we just have to create the space to help them get there.'

'Without judgement,' Nathan said sheepishly.

'Right again. There's a phrase I often remind myself about. It's called *unconditional positive regard*. It's just a fancy way of saying *no judgement* but on a deeper level. Basically, it's a reminder to me to regard the person before me in a positive regard — unconditionally. So no matter what they say or have done I don't jump to judgement; it's a safe space to resolve problems. Do you remember how I approached that conversation with Ciara?'

Nathan back rolled his memory and tied it to the G.R.O.W. model. 'Well,' he said hesitantly. 'First, you helped her define the problem. Then you asked her what an ideal solution would be and finally you encouraged her to come up with a few options.'

'Yep, pretty straightforward stuff, if you think about it. Just keep in mind where you are in the conversation and ensure you cover all the sections and you'll be able to have well-rounded coaching conversations.'

Nathan was nodding to himself as he replayed the scenario in his mind. Ultimately the goal is to resolve the problem. That's why Fionn didn't berate Ciara; this would've just shut things down. Nathan made a mental note to hold no judgement when his team made mistakes or came to him with a problem.

'There's one other thing that might be useful for you to be aware of. It's important to ensure that these conversations are just that, conversations. If the person begins to think that you're using a technique on them they may start to hold back. So what I suggest is to come with at least three different ways of asking for the same information for each stage of the model. Three for uncovering the Goal, three for diving deeper into the Reality, and so on.'

'Thanks,' said Nathan. 'That's really useful. I'll do that.'

Fionn called to Ciara. Even though she was only a few metres ahead, Ciara couldn't hear him over the wind. Fionn trotted forward and they stopped to discuss the situation. There was obviously still no sign of Stephen. While Fionn and Ciara talked through options, Nathan rubbed his aching knee before reaching into his pocket to pull out his phone and frantically capture everything he could remember about the coaching leadership style.

The Affiliate

He always believed it was important to keep a professional distance.

They were on the move again. Nathan could see Fionn was more than a little concerned. Clearly, he wasn't happy that they weren't able to find Stephen. He was either injured, or worse, or sitting in some pub somewhere regaling tales of survival to the locals unaware that he had been reported missing. Nathan hoped for the latter, but it was the least likely. He couldn't imagine having to spend the night out here in these conditions. The temperature had dropped another couple of degrees since they started out. *Unless he's got some sort of survival gear he's going to be in a world of hurt right now.*

'Do you think we'll find him?' asked Nathan.

Fionn looked up. 'Maybe, we've still got a couple of kilometres to go until we reach the car park. Because the fog is so thick we could easily have passed him on the way up without even realising it.'

Nathan could tell he was doing his best to be optimistic but Nathan could read the look of concern on his face. You can't not communicate, he reminded himself.

'Fancy teaching me more about the leadership styles?' asked Nathan as he tried to distract Fionn from his musings.

'Sure,' he said. 'Which one are we on? Ah, yes. The Affiliative Leadership Style. Okay, you know the routine, why is it useful and when would you use it?'

'This one stumps me. Is it about being affiliated with a group, your peers for example?' Nathan asked.

'This one tends to trip people up the most. It's simply about building strong relationships with others. This is true for your peers and also for your team. This style of leadership is valuable because it builds trust and cohesion, increases morale and opens up communication. Most importantly it can repair trust when it has been lost.' Fionn paused to let this last point sink in.

Nathan turned to look at him, his stubble scraping against the side of his hood. 'This one would be useful for me then,' Nathan said then laughed.

'I think so!' The two friends laughed. It reminded Nathan that he needed to do this more often — have more laughter in his life. Surely, he could get stuff done while he relaxed. This would certainly ease some of the tension at work.

Fionn interrupted Nathan's thoughts. 'So you'd use this style when the team is in disharmony, or if, for whatever reason, there's low trust in the environment. It's also really effective when the team is going through a stressful time, and, of course, it can heal rifts that might exist in the team.'

Nathan couldn't let go of the realisation that he was the cause of the problems within the team. Clearly, they didn't trust him and this was the root cause of the problems.

'This is useful,' said Nathan as he refocused. 'So the Affiliative leader would have to be good at building relationships, have large capital with others, be good at collaboration, and be friendly. That kind of thing.'

'Yep, that's right. They have high empathy and are very good at resolving conflict. They tend to shy away from conflict with others; however, they're very good at mediating a conflict between others.' Fionn paused for a moment, he could see Nathan was soaking up everything he was saying. 'What do you think are some of the challenges of an Affiliative leader?'

'Well that's obvious, isn't it? Getting too close to the team. Getting all buddy-buddy and blurring the line between manager and friend.'

'That's right. A strongly affiliative leader tends to value the relationship over performance, and so they don't call things out when standards start to drop or goals aren't met. It's a tough balance but an important one to get right.'

'Hmmm … it certainly is,' said Nathan. He was really feeling out of his depth with the Affiliative Leadership Style. He always believed it was important to keep a professional distance; however, he could see how he took this to extremes and needed to implement some of what Fionn was talking about.

'So how would you do that?'

Fionn chuckled. 'Well, a simple way I've used in the past is to sit down with the person and say something along the lines of, 'Thanks a million for your time, I know how busy you are. I wanted to have a chat and in order to do this I need to take off my friend hat and put on my manager hat', and as I'm saying this I mimic the actions. It's done a little tongue in cheek, but people get it. It sets up the right mindset for the conversation. And then, when the conversation is over I say, 'Now, I'll just take this hat off and put this one back on', all done with a cheeky smile on my face.'

Nathan laughed. As silly as it seemed he could see how this would work.

'It's really important to be able to have the tough conversations but it's equally important to ensure that the relationship is on solid ground first, otherwise the person's focus tends to be more on your relationship rather than on the words themselves. I know you want to talk about feedback so we'll talk about this some more in that context.'

'This is really useful,' said Nathan, almost absent-mindedly. His mind was consumed by his own situation at work and how much understanding the Affiliative Leadership Style would have made his transition into leadership so much easier. Then the realisation hit him.

'Claudia is an Affiliative leader!' he blurted out. 'That's her natural style. She's so good at building relationships. She can even have a heated argument with someone and it's weirdly okay. It's like her super power.'

Fionn laughed. 'So how is Claudia's style adding to your difficulties working with the team?'

Nathan was taken aback by the question. Claudia had been nothing but supportive; she was the one who hired him after all and the amount of patience she had shown was almost Herculean. But then it dawned on him.

'The team keep going to Claudia with their problems. Mostly about me, I imagine, but also with other things too.' Nathan thought some more. 'This is making it difficult for the team to make the break from her leadership to mine. Hmmm …' Nathan trailed off as his thoughts took over.

Fionn jumped in. 'It sounds like Claudia's a wonderful person and a great boss. It also sounds as if she's unaware of how her style is impacting your transition into your team leadership role. She's just doing what she's always done, supporting people and because she's an Affiliative leader this makes her feel good. What do you think needs to happen here?'

'I think I need to have an open conversation with Claudia when I get back.'

'I think that's a good idea; however, it also sounds like you've got some foundational work to do with the team first, or at least at the same time.'

'You're right,' said Nathan, feeling better about the trip home. He was starting to create a roadmap in his mind, a roadmap to becoming a better leader. Then it hit him. Being an Affiliative leader was great in theory, but how do you actually go about doing it? He had no idea.

'This might seem like a dumb question but …' Nathan trailed off in embarrassment.

'How do you do it?' interjected Fionn. 'It's not dumb at all. So you and I can have open honest conversations where we share things about what's going on in each other's lives and even though it might feel a little uncomfortable when we're sharing, we know we can trust each other not to judge and to keep confidences, right?'

'Of course! We've had our fair share of heart to hearts. We've had our disagreements too though.'

They both laughed at this.

'All relationships do, but what makes it safe to have these disagreements and to share confidences is trust.'

Nathan nodded.

'But it wasn't always like this, was it?' asked Fionn. 'We didn't just miraculously trust one another from day one.'

Nathan remembered back to when he first met Fionn. He was in week two of a fitness and leisure diploma in Sallynoggin. He remembered Fionn joining the course late and in the middle of a communication class, ironically. Fionn walked in with such confidence, spoke briefly to the lecturer and sat at one of the front tables. But that's not what he remembered most. What struck him was when Fionn turned around to the rest of the class, who, like Nathan were all staring at the back of his head wondering who this guy was, and he smiled confidently, made eye contact and nodded a friendly smile. *How could you not like a guy like that?*

'No, it takes a while to build a relationship. It starts off fairly standoffish at first; you know, talk about the weather and stuff.' Fionn laughed. 'That's right, but things change when one party shares a little about themselves; something personal that the other person doesn't yet know. This tends to make it easier for the other person to then share something about themselves. This is how vulnerability trust is built. Now, I'm not talking about *oversharing,*' Fionn stressed this point. 'Think of it like an onion. Think of going a couple of layers deep until more trust is built, and then, depending on how things progress, maybe going a layer deeper and so on. It's really not necessary to go to the core. That stuff is saved for our deeply personal relationships.'

Nathan nodded. This was making complete sense and is exactly what Claudia does; she's a master at it. *I wonder if she's even aware that she's doing it.*

'You used a phrase there a moment ago that sounds important. You said vulnerability trust. What's that about?' Nathan asked.

'In the workplace there are two types of trust. The first type is predictability trust. For example, if I asked you to deliver a task by a particular date and time and you agreed, predictability trust tells me that you will do it. I trust that you have the skills and attitude to deliver. That's predictability trust and it's made up of five subcomponents — I call it SC^4.'

Nathan laughed. 'SC^4? That's pretty fancy. What does it stand for?'

Fionn was smiling. 'Actually, I just made that up, but it's a clever way of remembering the parts to predictability trust. S stands for Sincerity. With sincerity the person believes that what they are saying is the truth but just because they are being sincere you don't have to believe them, you know. They can be sincerely wrong.'

They both laughed. 'But seriously,' the person might sincerely believe they are capable of completing a task; however, you might think otherwise. Now, you would never challenge a person's sincerity, that goes to the heart of who they are as a person. However, what if the person sincerely believes they can do the tasks, but you don't think they're there yet; they haven't quite got the skills. Which of the 4 C's might we be referring to here?'

Nathan thought for a moment. 'Capability?' he said.

'Yep,' replied Fionn. 'So they may not have the capability to perform the task ... *yet!*'

'You see, rather than telling the person you can't give them the task or project because you don't trust them, you can have a conversation with them about their capabilities. It might sound something like, 'I know you're really keen to take this on, but I'm not quite sure you're there *yet*. But how about you and I work together on those particular skills that might be required for a project like this so the next time an opportunity like this arises it will be a different conversation?''

Nathan was nodding. 'That sounds like a pretty positive conversation,' he said.

'Exactly, when we break down predictability trust, it's easier to have a conversation that allows us to move forward. What about this scenario? A person in your team is eager to help out. They always put up their hand wanting to take on more responsibilities; however, what you soon discover is the person keeps dropping the ball and missing important delivery dates. Their excuse is that they just have too much on?'

'That would be a Capacity issue,' said Nathan confidently.

'Spot on, so for this person they may be completely blind to the fact that they have too much on their plate, but their desire to please or get ahead is actually holding them back. So bringing this to their attention might be all that's required. If I can paraphrase Fritz Perls, "Sometimes awareness is curative". Another issue with them failing to deliver might be their inability to estimate their work. Maybe they were never taught this skill and it's all guess work for them. Do you have a way of estimating their work?'

Nathan was caught on the hop. 'Hmmm … not really, I guess I just guess.'

'Here's a traditional way project managers estimate a task. Ask the person how long they think a task will take; let's call that M for most likely. Then ask them if everything goes perfectly with no obstacles how long will it take them then; let's call that O for optimistic. Lastly, we ask them to consider how long it will take if everything goes wrong; we call that P for pessimistic. Then we throw it into a simple formula: $(O + 4M + P) / 6$.'

'Simple! Are you kidding me!'

Fionn laughed again. 'It's only tricky because you're trying to do it in your head. I'll write it out for you when we get back. The formula is useful, but here's the key to helping the person deliver more effectively and to become better at estimating their work. In order for them to give you the optimistic estimate (O) they have to make assumptions, so we ask them what assumptions they will make. The same is true for the pessimistic estimate (P); they have to consider the risks associated with the task, so ask them what these are. Now, it's your job to ensure that as many of the assumptions they made come true and it's up to you to reduce as many risks associated with the task are mitigated.'

'Okay, I see,' said Nathan thoughtfully. 'So rather than ask them just for a few numbers plucked out of the air they have to think a little more deeply, and me, as their manager, clear the way for them to succeed.'

'That's it.'

'But surely that seems a little overboard for every task.'

'It is a little, but you'd be surprised how quick it actually is. Remember though, the purpose is to help them think more deeply about how they estimate their work. A very simple way of estimating smaller tasks is to ask, what have you done in the past that was of similar complexity? How long did that take?'

'So really it's about getting them to think about it a little deeper before offering up a number.'

'Yep, that's it. If they keep dropping the ball that might be a great opportunity for a coaching conversation.' Fionn turned to Nathan and winked.

Nathan smiled in return. 'So we've done Sincerity, Capability, and Capacity. What about the other two C's?'

'The third C stands for Consistency. So, for example, imagine I was working for you and one week I was shit-hot. I was on fire, I was smashing through the work, and then, the following week I was hopeless. I was grumpy, my work was lacklustre with many obvious holes, but then a few days later I was on fire again.'

'I'd say you weren't very consistent.'

'That's it! Consistency is the third C. So what are your thoughts about how you'd approach this one?'

Nathan gave it some thought. 'I'm not sure. It sounds like a tricky one. I wonder if there is something going on in their personal life that maybe having an impact on their work.'

'Well, listen to you getting all empathetic and stuff.'

They both laughed. 'But you're right. This can be a tricky conversation because the person might be having trouble in a personal relationship or have experienced a loss they haven't shared with you. They could have a mood disorder like anxiety or depression, or they may be on medication, or be experiencing an undiagnosed hormone imbalance, or they might have a substance abuse issue. It's impossible to know. We have to tread carefully with this one.

'Of course,' Fionn went on, 'It could be that they were up all night playing video games or watching Netflix. It might be a simple conversation; regardless though, the conversation needs to be had so we can help them become more consistent because if you're noticing it you can be sure the team is noticing it too.'

Nathan nodded pensively. 'Nice one. What about the last C?'

'The last C is a bit of stretch being a C,' Fionn said and then laughed. 'The last C refers to Care. You know, does the person have the right sense of care to be given the task?'

'You mean the right sense of quality?' asked Nathan.

'Yeah, I told you it was a stretch.' Fionn laughed again. 'Sometimes good enough is good enough; however, there are going to be times when something has to be one hundred per cent accurate. Think of the accountant who just can't go home in the evening because the million dollar balance sheet is out by two dollars. That's the type of care we're talking about. But, like I said, it doesn't have to be for every task. Sometimes good enough is good enough.'

'Wow!' said Nathan. 'I never thought there was so much to trust.'

'They're just ways of breaking down things in your mind to have conversations about performance. Stephen Covey has just two forms of predictability trust; competence and character. That's it. Is the person good at what they do and do they have the right type of character, one that builds trust?'

Nathan was thinking about his own team and where they fall down on the different areas of trust. Fionn interrupted his thoughts.

'Before you start thinking about where your team fits into this trust model think about yourself first. Where do you fall down in these areas?'

Nathan felt confronted, but Fionn was right. During this entire experience Fionn was holding up a mirror, which allowed Nathan to see where he was going wrong, and how he could do better. He put his ego in check and thought about the question.

He felt he was sincere about his work and his communications; the problem he now realised was that this was being clouded by his temperament. *I wonder what Stephen Covey would say about my character?* Clearly, he had to work on this. He did care about his team and he did want to make the environment the kind of place that people wanted to be a part of. Wasn't that what leadership was about, after all?

In reality, he was just a first-time manager and he was finding out how much experience actually counts. You can't fake this stuff, he reminded himself. So when it comes to Capability, he thought, he was probably on the lower end and humility is something he needed to practise some more. He needed to listen and be more patient with his team.

Regarding Capacity, he didn't really know. He found that he was constantly busy, but he wasn't sure how he was adding any value. If he was asked what he actually did from one day to the next, he could probably talk in generalisations but could offer nothing specific. He reminded himself that he needed to do that delegation exercise Fionn suggested; writing things down would give him a better idea of where his time went.

He thought about Consistency and it became clear that he was consistently grumpy, consistently in a bad mood, consistently picking up on everything the team did and didn't do. At least he was consistent, he joked to himself. *This needs to change.*

Lastly, there was Care. Maybe his sense of care was too much. Not in the real meaning of the word; his team would probably say he didn't care, but in terms of quality maybe he needed to back off, to put that perfectionist mindset behind him. Everyone makes mistakes and no small children are going to die because of anything we do, as Claudia often reminded him.

Nathan let out a big sigh. Fionn, who was respectfully silent, turned to him. 'Is everything alright?'

'Yeah, I'm just realising how much work I have to do to win back the trust of the team.'

'It's an ongoing thing, my friend. Besides, if this was easy everyone would be doing it. We'd have more scout leaders than scouts. Being a scout is relatively easy; being a scout leader is hard.'

'You're not kidding. So what about vulnerability trust? Is that any easier to understand than predictability trust?'

Fionn laughed. 'Well, yes and no,' he said with a grin. 'You see, vulnerability trust takes courage. Vulnerability trust exists in a team when a person feels safe enough to put their hand up and say, 'I messed up', and she knows that the team won't criticise, condemn or blame. Or a team member confesses that he is out of his depth and needs help. It's uncomfortable to do this, but he knows the team won't judge him and he'll get the support he needs. Vulnerability trust is present when a team member feels she can challenge the views of the entire team without the fear of backlash, ridicule or derision. Does all that make sense?'

'I think so,' said Nathan. He was thinking how this is the exact opposite of his team. At team meetings people don't speak up or share ideas for fear of being shot down or laughed at. *God, team meetings are painful,* he thought.

Fionn went on, as if reading his thoughts. 'Without vulnerability trust, people don't feel safe to admit mistakes, they don't feel safe to challenge, or to innovate. In fact, when something goes wrong in a low-trust environment people are more likely to make excuses, sweep things under the carpet or blame others because they think, or even know, they'll be punished. As you can imagine, this creates a dog-eat-dog environment where everyone is out for themselves. A team like this would be very toxic and unhealthy.'

Fionn paused and Nathan took the opportunity to let that thought sink in. Fionn could've been describing his own team. Yeah, they laughed and joked among themselves from time to time, but there was an underlying sense of tension that Nathan could never put his finger on … until now.

'You know, one of my favourite authors describes this beautifully,' Fionn said. 'Patrick Lencioni believes that every team has the potential to experience five dysfunctions. In his aptly named book *The Five Dysfunctions of a Team,* he sees vulnerability trust as the first and arguably the most important function to get right. From his work he noticed that if a team is in trouble and you wind back the clock about six to nine months there is always an underlying cause, that in the beginning, is imperceptible but seems to be the root cause of larger problems over time. Any guesses what that is?'

'Might it be vulnerability trust?'

'Ha! Ha! ... why yes, young man, it would be exactly that. You see, without vulnerability there is only invulnerability; the idea that we don't make mistakes which is a fallacy even for the most perfect person. As a leader, if we give off this sense that "I don't make mistakes or mistakes aren't tolerated" this sets up an environment of low trust and ultimately blame. Not a nice place to be in.'

Nathan was nodding.

'But it gets worse. Because when there is no trust there can be no conflict. I mean healthy conflict here; the type of conflict in which a team vigorously discusses and debates the issues on the table. They are hard on the problem but soft on the people to paraphrase Stephen Covey. They never allow things to get personal. That way the best ideas bubble to the surface, right? If the debate is safe and unencumbered by the fear of being dismissed outright then ultimately the best ideas, the most innovative ideas, end up being the ones the team runs with. It's a pretty exciting position to be in for a team. No more boring meetings.' Fionn laughed. 'Because without conflict there is a false harmony. People pretend to get on, pretend to agree, pretend to tow the company line, but in reality they are just staying quiet because it's easier. Disagreements are never resolved, they're ignored or pushed away so we get on with things. The problem with this is that they tend to leak out ... over about six to nine months.' Fionn was laughing again.

Nathan thought he was having way too much fun sharing his knowledge while every word cut a deeper realisation of the problems he and his team was facing and they probably weren't even aware of it.

'But there's more!' Fionn was on a roll. 'Without healthy conflict there can be no commitment; not really. It's only when everyone feels like they have a voice, when they feel they've had a chance to debate the issue and they've genuinely been heard that they are likely to buy into the final decision ... even if it's not the decision that they would've made. A lack of commitment leads to confusion and a team's commitment to key decisions is essential for performance.'

'I always follow Lencioni's advice to instil the following rule with the team: *It's not consensus we're after, it's commitment.* With a large team you're never going to get agreement from everyone, but that's okay; the debates are what are important to shape the idea. However, once everyone has been heard a decision has to be made and once it has been made I expect everyone to get on board.' Fionn paused. 'Does this make sense?'

'Yeah, I think so.' Nathan's mind was processing as much of this as he could. So far they were up to the third dysfunction and he was keen to get them all but he hoped they would stop for a break shortly so he could capture everything in his notes app. He wanted more though.

'Okay, what are the other two dysfunctions of a team?'

'As you've seen so far, each dysfunction leads to the next. The same is true for the final two because without commitment there can be no real accountability and a lack of accountability leads to low standards. *Good excuses,*' Fionn stressed. 'But low standards. And, of course, low standards lead to poor team performance. It is more likely to lead to ego-driven individualised performance but certainly not a collective team performance.

That's the last dysfunction, poor results.' Fionn paused and Nathan digested this last pearl of wisdom.

'Ultimately,' that's what we're in business for; to deliver results. Our job as leaders is to create an environment in which everyone can thrive, not only as individuals but collectively as a team. A high-performing team will always outshine a team of high-performing individuals.'

'There's a lot to it, isn't there?' said Fionn. 'In some ways, the Affiliative Leadership Style is the easiest to understand but probably the most difficult to implement.'

Nathan's head was down as he nodded in agreement. Caught up in his thoughts he accidentally walked into the back of Ciara who had stopped to double-check her bearings.

'Sorry,' Nathan said to Ciara. His apology went unanswered, which made Nathan feel a bit shit. Clearly, Ciara wasn't happy with having him along.

Fionn and Ciara conferred over the map, and after brushing off Ciara's rebuke, Nathan dropped to one knee, shucked off his rucksack, took out his phone and furiously captured everything he could remember.

The Flash of Light

Stop! Don't run.

Nathan finished capturing everything he could remember from his earlier conversation with Fionn. His knee continued to ache and grew more painful with each step. He was glad they were on their way back down the hill although he found going downhill made the pain worse. He pressed his thumb into the tendon above the knee; paradoxically the pain he felt from the rubbing seemed to ease the underlying ache. Fionn and Ciara continued to pour over the map.

Nathan stood up and stretched as he enjoyed a respite from the weight of his rucksack. It was then that something caught his eye. The fog parted for a brief moment and Nathan could've sworn he saw a flash of a light in the darkness. It came and went in the blink of an eye. He continued to train his attention in that direction, willing the wind to separate the fog for just an instant. Fionn and Ciara had finished their planning, and he could hear the rustling of their coats as they hauled on their rucksacks.

'Okay,' said Fionn. 'Ready for the last push?'

Nathan heard the words, but they sounded as if they were coming from far away. Suddenly, he saw it again; the fog parted and the light flashed, just for a moment, but it was enough. Without hesitating and keeping his eye trained in the direction of where the light was coming from he took off in that direction. With each footfall his knee screamed at him, but he pushed the pain to the back of his mind. Behind him he could hear Fionn and Ciara shouting, the wind carrying their words.

'Stop! Don't run.'

The words didn't make sense to Nathan. Of course he was going to run. He'd found him, he'd found Stephen. At least he thought he had. The fog was thickening again and the light disappeared. He pushed on. Surely he must be close by now. He stopped in his tracks. Perhaps he'd imagined it. Perhaps his fatigue had finally caught up with him. His chest heaved and his breath, briefly illuminated by his headlamp, was absorbed into the fog. He turned his head in the direction of Fionn and Ciara, their headlamps appeared briefly before disappearing again in the fog.

And then he heard it. His head whipped around. Was it the wind? Perhaps his imagination was playing with him. He heard it again. Over the bellowing of the wind he heard a faint cry. He headed in the direction of the voice that was calling out, and then he saw it. A headlamp; the sound of the cries was growing louder.

'Please help me!' He could hear the pain and exhaustion in the man's voice and then he was on him. Nathan dropped to his knees next to the man who reached out and grabbed his arm. He was lying on his back with his left leg bent at the knee, his right leg was straight out in front of him. His body was shaking uncontrollably and in the light of the head torch the man's lips were blue.

'Thank you! Thank you! Ah, thank you so much.' The man collapsed back onto the soft earth and rested against his day pack which he had removed earlier. He was still shaking. He closed his eyes tightly as he fought back the pain. Nathan glanced down at his leg and noticed something sticking through the man's rain protection trousers.

Fionn and Ciara arrived at exactly the same time. Ciara dropped Nathan's rucksack next to him while Fionn focused his attention on the man.

'Are you Stephen?' asked Fionn, clearly taking control of the situation.

'Yes,' said the man through chattering teeth. 'Yes, I'm Stephen.'

'I'm Fionn. We're the mountain rescue team. You're going to be alright.'

Fionn had already taken off his rucksack and was rummaging through the side pocket. He produced a small silver packet and handed it to Nathan.

'Here,' he said. 'He's suffering from hypothermia and we need to keep him as warm as possible. Open this and put it over his torso, as tightly as you can.'

'Ciara!' shouted Fionn. 'We're going to have to carry him out. Unpack the stretcher.'

Ciara was standing over them both staring as if in shock.

'Ciara!' said Fionn again, louder this time. 'We need to move. Get the stretcher out.'

As if responding to a starter's pistol, Ciara sprang into action. Fionn turned his attention back to Stephen, who continued to shake.

'Fionn,' said Nathan as Fionn continued to rummage in his rucksack.

'Fionn!' said Nathan again. 'I think it's his leg.'

'What is?' replied Fionn, distracted. Then he leant over Stephen and spoke in a raised voice. 'Stephen, can you hear me?'

Stephen nodded weakly. 'I need you to stay awake, do you hear me?' Again he nodded, his teeth continued to chatter.

Nathan continued to hold the silver blanket over him as best he could as he battled against the wind. Fionn continued to talk loudly to Stephen. 'Are you allergic to anything, Stephen? Are you allergic to Paracetamol? I need to give you something to help with the pain.'

'No! No!' The words came out in little staccato bursts.

'Fionn,' Nathan tried again. 'He'll need more than Paracetamol.'

Fionn looked at Nathan. Nathan turned his head towards Stephen's leg and Fionn's eyes followed the beam of light that lit up the white protrusion against the darkness. Stephen's tibia stuck out from his rain trousers like a pointy iceberg rising up from a dark ocean.

'Oh Christ!' Fionn pushed Nathan out of the way to get a closer look. The silver blanket rose up in the wind and Nathan grabbed it just in time. Stephen lay unresponsive.

'Should we try to push it back in?' asked Nathan.

'God no!' said Fionn as he gently cut away Stephen's rain proofs. 'I need you to give Stephen those painkillers.' Fionn nodded in the direction of the first-aid kit on the ground next to his rucksack. There's water in the side pocket. 'Oh Christ!' Fionn said again as he crouched close to the wound. 'Okay, the majority of the bleeding has subsided,' said Fionn more to himself than anyone else. 'That's good news. It means it hasn't ruptured an artery. Besides,' he continued lowering his voice and leaning into Nathan. 'He'd be dead by now if that was the case.'

Nathan lifted Stephen's head as Fionn continued to examine the wound as best he could with his head torch, which was the only light available.

'Here,' said Nathan softly. 'Take these.' Stephen opened his eyes and Nathan fed the painkillers directly into his mouth. He placed the water bottle against his chapped lips and Stephen coughed as water sputtered across his cheeks.

'Here, take another sip,' said Nathan. Stephen raised his head and drank some more. This time more successfully, and using what seemed like the last of his strength, nodded his head slowly to indicate he had swallowed the pain killers.

Behind them Ciara continued to wrestle with the telescopic stretcher and swearing softly in frustration. Nathan wondered if she was aware of the gravity of Stephen's injuries.

Fionn reached past him and pulled the first-aid kit closer to Stephen's leg. He straightened his leg as gently and slowly as humanly possible. Stephen grimaced but didn't cry out. It was only when Fionn let out a sigh that Nathan realised he too was holding his breath.

'What are you doing,' asked Nathan. 'Shouldn't we cover the break?'

'That's what I'm doing,' said Fionn as he reached into the first-aid kit and pulled out a large bandage and placed it between both of Stephen's legs at the level of the break. His hand disappeared into the first-aid kit again and he retrieved another large bandage. He unwound it, grabbed one end in a closed fist and started to wrap the bandage around his fist and around itself. His hands worked fast, and in the light of his torch, Nathan could see he was making a donut shape out of the bandage. He placed this above the break, grabbed another bandage and repeated the process. Nathan watched in silence. When the second donut was completed he placed this below the protruding bone.

'Now,' said Fionn. All we have to do is wrap this bandage over and around the break so it doesn't press down on the exposed bone.' Gently Fionn worked the bandage under both of Stephen's legs and over the top of the two donuts. 'His other leg will act as a splint.' As he held the bandage in place he reached into the first-aid kit once again, retrieved a couple of pins and secured the bandage tightly against the outside of Stephen's leg.

There was a resounding click behind them and Ciara stood triumphantly over the stretcher which was fully assembled and lay on the ground in front of her.

'What happened to his leg?' asked Ciara. She had been completely oblivious to what was going on; having been completely engrossed in assembling the stretcher.

Fionn ignored the question and leant over Stephen again. 'Stephen, can you hear me, buddy. I need you to stay awake now, okay?'

Stephen opened his eyes and nodded as best he could.

'Okay,' said Fionn, turning to Nathan and Ciara. 'We need to gently lift him onto the stretcher. I'll grab his legs. Nathan, you grab under his shoulders. Ciara, when we lift him, I want you to push the stretcher underneath him. Got it?' He looked at them both, holding their gaze until each nodded in agreement.

They got into position. 'Okay, on three. One, two, three,' said Fionn. He and Nathan lifted Stephen a few inches. Stephen let out a bone-chilling scream and Ciara quickly pushed the stretcher under him. They let him down gently and Stephen panted heavily through gritted teeth. Despite the cold his forehead was sweating and his skin was ashen white. Nathan tucked the silver blanket around him again, unsure how much it was actually helping.

'Sorry, Stephen,' said Fionn. 'That's the worst of it over now. We'll get you home soon.' He turned to Ciara and Nathan once again. 'I need you both to take the first shift carrying the stretcher. I'll quickly set our navigation and call the team to ready them for our arrival.' As he spoke he repacked his rucksack and zipped up the side pockets.

Nathan and Ciara nodded. All three grabbed their rucksacks, heaved them onto their shoulders and got into position. Nathan reached for Stephen's day pack.

'Leave it,' said Fionn. 'It'll be tough enough getting down the hill as it is.'

Nathan complied without question, bent his knees and gripped the handles at the end of the aluminium poles.

'Ready, lift,' said Ciara. Both of them lifted in unison and Nathan felt a stabbing pain in his knee. He grunted but pushed the pain to the back of his mind. He wished he had asked Fionn for a couple of the painkillers.

Fionn, having finalised their direction of travel, led the way. Nathan could hear him on the phone talking to Anna, he assumed. It was difficult to hear over the sound of the wind, but he heard the words ambulance and hypothermia.

'Thank you.' Nathan heard the words but wasn't paying attention. He was concentrating on his balance and trying to ignore the pain in his knee and the strain under his fingers.

'You saved my life,' Stephen said. Nathan looked down at him. Stephen was staring directly into his eyes. A tear rolled to the side of his face. 'I thought I was going to die.'

All of a sudden, a burst of emotion rushed through Nathan. The image of his father lying in his coffin — so small — so lifeless. The same thought repeated itself over and over in his mind, *That's it for him. That's it for him.* Tears filled his eyes and streamed down his face. He sniffed hard and looked straight ahead, his face screwed up with emotion. His breathing was wet with his sobs as he tried to hold back his grief. Finally, he gave up and his emotions flowed freely. He felt Stephen's hand grip his forearm. He gave it a reaffirming squeeze as if to say, *It's going to be alright.*

They marched for what seemed like an eternity. Gradually, Ciara and Nathan got into a good rhythm which made carrying the stretcher less jarring on his shoulders. His knee was almost numb with the pain, but his fingers screamed in agony. Fionn dropped back and walked next to him. He looked down and saw that Stephen was holding tightly onto Nathan's arm.

'Ready for a break?' he asked.

'I thought you'd never ask,' said Nathan with relief.

'Ciara,' Fionn raised his voice. 'Let's take a break.'

Nathan and Ciara stopped and Nathan followed Ciara's lead and lowered the stretcher to the ground. Ciara fell forward onto her hands and knees, and Nathan fell backwards holding his hands in front of his face. He tried to open his fingers but they protested and in the end he just held them against his chest.

'This is a holiday you won't forget in a hurry,' said Fionn.

Nathan grimaced as he sat back supported by his rucksack.

'How are you doing, Stephen,' asked Fionn.

'A bit shit, actually,' said Stephen.

Fionn laughed. 'I think you'll be fine.' He patted him reassuringly on the shoulder. 'We're not too far from the car park now. You can see the car lights in the distance.'

Stephen raised his head and nodded. 'Not long now, then.' He said as if to no one in particular.

Fionn sat next to Nathan and both stared in silence at the lights in the distance. Then Nathan saw something strange. He stared ahead and concentrated intently.

'Is that ...' his voice trailed off. 'Are those lights coming towards us?' he asked.

'The cavalry is on the way,' said Fionn gleefully. He had asked Anna to send up Sophie and Sienna who had returned to the car park an hour or so earlier.

'Oh, thank God!' said Nathan as he fell over on his side in relief.

The Connection

Lights flashed red and blue against the dark clouds.

The first thing Nathan did when they arrived back at the car park was retrieve Stephen's phone from his car. Although the signal was patchy, Stephen was able to chat briefly to his daughter to let her know he was okay and that he'd soon be at the hospital. As he stood at a distance, Nathan could see it was an emotional conversation. Although he couldn't hear what was being said he imagined the relief and love his daughter was expressing however many miles away.

'The ambulance will be here in about ten minutes,' Fionn said to everyone as he put his phone back in his pocket. He looked over at Nathan who was now sitting next to Stephen keeping him company. After layering him up with extra blankets, and being extra careful to avoid disturbing his leg, Anna got off her knees with a comforting smile for Stephen and approached the rest of the team. Nathan noticed Anna was shivering, which he thought was strange. She had on what looked like a good quality hill-walking coat and was wearing a woollen hat, but then he saw it. Her trousers from the knees down were soaking wet. The material must have been clinging to her skin and causing her body temperature to drop. Stephen thanked Anna and dropped his head back onto the rolled-up coat that acted as a makeshift pillow.

'What's the pain like, now?' Nathan asked.

'Oh, I'd say it's reduced to a level of agony.' Stephen laughed and Nathan couldn't help but join in. 'I'm just glad to be alive, my friend.' Stephen was looking into Nathan's eyes. The intensity of the emotion he saw there made him uncomfortable. He looked away to compose himself.

'Thank you,' said Stephen. The sound of the words catching in his throat made Nathan look back down at Stephen. Stephen's eyes were filled with tears now, but his eye contact remained as strong as before. Nathan was drawn into his gaze. A surge of emotion erupted from his chest and Stephen pulled him closer. Both men sobbed as they embraced. Nathan didn't fully understand why he was crying, but the release felt good.

Stephen released him from his embrace and Nathan looked around awkwardly. Everyone was busying themselves either packing up equipment or preparing for the arrival of the ambulance. Nathan dabbed away the tears from his eyes with his gloves.

'What was it like out there? Did you ever think we were going to find you?'

Stephen thought about the question for a moment. 'You know, when I broke my leg the pain was so intense that I blacked out for a while, and when I woke I didn't know where I was. When I realised my situation, I got really scared. It was dark, I was growing so cold from lying there and the rain was lashing down. I tried to think clearly, but the pain in my leg sapped me of any concentration. I couldn't move and I was at the mercy of God or the universe or whatever you believe in or don't believe in.' Stephen paused and a look of peace came over his face. 'And then, after a while things felt different, you know?' Stephen looked up at Nathan again. 'It's hard to explain, but there was a sense of calm. Even though my leg was still agony, it was like it wasn't part of me and my mind drifted to memories of my family, to the times in my life that I'm tremendously grateful for.' Stephen broke his gaze.

Lights flashed red and blue against the dark clouds. It was almost surreal watching the colourful lights approaching them silently through the darkness.

'I also thought about those times that I'm deeply ashamed of,' Stephen added then he looked at Nathan. 'And you know what? They were times when I mistreated people or took them for granted. When I made a big deal of things and walked over other people's feelings because it made me feel more powerful. I realised that even though I have achieved a lot, even though I am wealthy by many peoples' standards, I am alone. I realised that I am the poorest person in the world.'

Stephen fell silent and Nathan thought about the death of his father. Was he scared? Did he think of the happy times and those things he was grateful for? Were his last minutes on this earth tortured by memories of guilt and regret? The inability to make them right?

The headlights of the ambulance swept into the car park and knocked Nathan out of his trance. He looked down at Stephen who was staring up at him. Tears streamed down Nathan's face. He already had so much regret in his life. Stephen reached up and squeezed Nathan's arm and pulled him into another embrace and he sobbed into the injured man's shoulder.

The sound of footsteps crunching towards them broke the moment and Nathan looked away into the darkness to compose himself. If Fionn noticed anything he didn't let on.

'Okay, Stephen,' he said with enthusiasm. 'Let's get you into the ambulance and give you something a little stronger for the pain.'

The driver of the ambulance manoeuvred the vehicle so it backed towards Stephen, who continued to lie prostrate on the portable stretcher. When it came to a stop the back doors opened and two paramedics jumped out. The inside of the ambulance consisted of all the equipment you'd see on a medical drama. Everything neatly compartmentalised for easy access. The paramedics pulled out a stretcher and introduced themselves to Stephen. Nathan stood back and let them do their thing. Everything was very professional and Stephen found himself wrapped up and ready to be hoisted into the back of the ambulance in no time.

The two paramedics lifted the stretcher in unison and paused at Stephen's command.

'Wait,' he said. Turning his head towards Nathan, he reached out his hand. Nathan approached him and both men grasped hands tightly. Stephen looked meaningfully into Nathan's eyes. 'Thank you,' he said. With an extra squeeze, he released his grip and was lifted gently into the back of the ambulance. Nathan watched as they secured him in place. Stephen was chatting happily as if nothing at all had happened. Nathan didn't know Stephen before the incident, but he could recognise that he was a changed man. An uncomfortable feeling rose in Nathan; a feeling he couldn't quite put his finger on. It disappeared almost as quickly as it had appeared and Nathan pushed it to the back of his mind.

The Commander

That's why it's so important to have strong relationships in the first place.

D id you pick them?' asked Fionn over the sound of the car's air conditioning as it blasted out heat. They were sitting next to one another. The headlights lit up the car park and the shadows of the team lengthened and shortened as they busied themselves packing up the remainder of the gear. Nathan took a sip of his tea and enjoyed the feeling of the hot liquid as it warmed his stomach. *Warmth,* he thought to himself. *Something I'll never take for granted again.*

Now that the adrenaline of the evening had faded the pain in his knee became pretty intense. He was sitting with one leg out of his trousers with a chemical ice-pack strapped to the outside of his knee. It was nothing serious or even permanent, Fionn had said. It was caused by the iliotibial band, the long band of tissue that runs from your hip to just below your knee, rubbing over a fluid-filled sack called a bursa, which caused it to become inflamed. Even though it could be extremely painful when overused, with a bit of ice and rest, it would be back to normal in no time. Nathan had no reason to doubt Fionn's diagnosis, and besides, sitting in the warmth of the car drinking a hot cup of tea was better than running around outside in the wind and drizzle. *Good old Irish weather,* he joked to himself.

'Did I pick what?' asked Nathan.

'You have two more of the leadership styles.'

Nathan was taken aback. 'What do you mean?'

'When we found Stephen did you not notice a change in pace, the sense of urgency?'

'Of course,' said Nathan. 'You mean that was deliberate?'

'Absolutely! It was clear that Ciara was out of her depth, and that's fine, she's still learning; and you, acting like John Wayne tearing off in the direction of the headlamp without any concern for your own well-being. Someone had to take control and I did it in a very deliberate way.'

Nathan was a little offended. 'What do you mean, I was acting like John Wayne?'

Fionn softened his tone. 'What I mean is, what if you had rolled your ankle on the uneven ground. It was dark and there's no way you could see underfoot. To be honest, I count us lucky that didn't happen. Could you imagine the situation we'd have been in if we had to try and carry you out too.'

'Oh yeah,' said Nathan, a little sheepishly. 'I see what you mean.' He took another sip of his tea and avoided eye contact for a moment.

'It's all good in the hood. The main thing is we were able to bring Stephen back to his family. Mission completed.' Fionn laughed.

'So, tell me more about the leadership styles you just mentioned. I'm assuming they were the Pace-Setting and Commanding Styles because there was very little democracy out there.' They both laughed.

'You're damn right there was very little democracy out there,' Fionn replied. 'In an emergency the worst thing we can do is put things out for a vote. That's when the Commanding Style kicks in; this style builds engagement by soothing fears and giving clear direction in an emergency. Even though it's the least effective style in most situations and is largely the most damaging of all the styles, it has its place and that's when there's an emergency — when decisions need to be made and made quickly. There's always a risk of relationship collateral damage, but the benefits outweigh these. That's why it's so important to have strong relationships in the first place. You need some credit in the bank to be able to pull it off and this style of leadership cannot be your default. If it is, it will decimate a team.' Fionn paused to let this sink in and for good reason too. Nathan recognised that this was his go-to style.

'This style undermines the ability to give people the sense that their job fits into a grand, shared mission. It leads to people feeling less committed or even alienated from their jobs and thinking, 'Why does any of this matter?' The Commanding Style comes from the old military command and control hierarchies used in the twentieth century … interestingly enough, this style is now even cross-pollinated with other styles in the modern military,' Fionn added.

'What do you mean cross-pollinated?'

'After 9/11, when America went into Iraq and especially Afghanistan they recognised, very quickly, that they were losing the *war on terror*. Even though they had the most money to invest in the best equipment and best training; even though they had the best communications' equipment and the best weapons, they were consistently finding themselves on the back foot. They found the enemy could move much faster than they could and they found themselves constantly reacting, and instead of making progress, they were going backwards.

'It wasn't long before they recognised it wasn't more money that they needed, or guns or better training; they recognised that they needed to change their organisational structure. They needed to change how decisions were being made and how they operated as a team. You see, believe it or not, there were very well-defined silos in the American Army at the time and everyone stayed in their lanes, which was a huge barrier to communication. It slowed everything down, and information, if it was passed along at all, was often incomplete and useless.

'When it came to decision-making, the information was passed up the chain of command where the decision was made by the person who was furthest away from action. Then that decision was passed back down to be executed. You can see why they were failing. The Al Qaeda, in small units, were able to pop up, cause some damage and disappear again before the Americans knew what was happening. So, even though they didn't have the same degree of military training as the Americans, even though they didn't have the money, the resources or the weapons, they were still able to wreak havoc.' Fionn paused.

Nathan's thumbs were moving at lightning speed over the digital keyboard on his iPhone. After a moment, he stopped. 'Phew,' he said. 'Got it!'

'Here's an important point to remember.' Fionn paused for effect. 'It's very rarely resources that stop people or teams from being successful, it's resourcefulness.' Fionn paused again. 'How is it you can have these small companies, which were literally started by kids in their parents' garages, taking on the behemoths of an industry? They have no money, but they have resourcefulness and within a few years they are dominating the market.'

Nathan finished typing and raised his iPhone. 'Case in point,' he said with a smile.

'Exactly, but let's get back to the military.'

Nathan jokingly poised his thumbs over his iPhone. 'Ready,' he said, smiling again.

'The military focused on breaking down silos, breaking down the traditional M.E.C.E. approach to organisational structure.' Fionn glanced over at Nathan's screen and corrected him. 'No, it's not Mecca, it's M-E-C-E. It stands for Mutually Exclusive Collectively Exhaustive. Basically, it's something that everyone buys into, but everyone recognises that it ultimately doesn't work. The vertical approach to organisational structure simply doesn't work by design.

'Think about it,' he said. 'If I asked you, 'Who is your first team? Who is your number one team?' What would you say?'

Nathan thought for a minute. 'I guess my first team is the team I lead. The developers and testers and so on.'

'And that's what most people would say, but it's *wrong.*' Fionn dragged out the word wrong as if he was from a country farm in Idaho or somewhere in the American Midwest. 'If your direct reports are your first team, where are you likely to spend most of your time?'

'Well, with my direct reports.'

'That's right! Your focus would be vertically downward. Earlier we talked about the Affiliative Leadership Style and why this style of leadership is so important for building trust. I wasn't only referring to building trust with your direct team, I was referring to building trust across the organisation and especially with your peers. This is essential because you have no authoritative influence over your peers, you do over your team but not your peers. Therefore, if anyone at the leadership table doesn't agree with the idea of another leader they might debate it for a while but then decide to encourage their team to do what they've always done, which in the majority of instances, is to look after themselves, to put themselves first over the needs of other teams and over the collective needs of the organisation. Again, all this leads to silos.' Fionn paused to let Nathan catch up. 'Your first team must always be that of your peers because that's where the tough conversations have to occur. That's where the ideas are vigorously debated before a final decision is passed to the team. Collectively. With one voice. This can only happen if there are strong bonds of trust between each person; when each person recognises that they are debating an issue for the overall benefit of the organisation and not debating each other. They firmly recognise that having different views is okay, and being able to engage in a little conflict, around an issue, is actually healthy for a team. I'll talk more about this a little later. I can see the team is nearly ready for the debrief, but I wanted to share with you what the military did to speed up their decision-making capability.'

Nathan nodded.

'Ultimately what they did was to push the responsibility for making decisions down to the person closest to the action. After all, they have the most information at that point. They recognised they would need to train their people to consider other aspects of the environment, so it's an informed decision, and they also recognised that mistakes were going to happen. When this occurred they made sure the lessons from these mistakes were captured and communicated widely across the teams. There was no punishment, only learning.

'Lastly, what they did was actively break down the silos by introducing the concept of networking; individuals from different teams worked closely together, to share what they needed to do their jobs and the cross-pollinated teams did their best to support each other. What these changes led to was a huge turnaround in information gathering and response times. For the first time since the war started they were able to get onto the front foot and start making inroads into dismantling Al Qaeda. And we know how well that worked out for them, don't we?' said Fionn laughing as he opened the door. A rush of cold air hit Nathan.

'Even though things didn't work out for the American military in the end because of other complicating factors, the change in organisational structure and mindset was the right thing to do.'

Nathan nodded and went to pull his leg through his other trouser leg when Fionn stopped him. 'Sorry buddy, this is a closed-door meeting. These debriefs can be … well, honest and confronting. I won't be long. While I'm gone expand on your thinking about the Commanding leader. What do you think is required for the Commanding leader to soften their edges a bit and become more effective? Also, flesh out the Pace-Setter style as well. Think about it in terms of what you've experienced both now and in the past. You know more about this stuff than you give yourself credit for; the trick is to turn it into something practical and useful. I'll be back soon. With that, Fionn closed the door and made his way the short distance across the parking lot where he was greeted by a steaming cup of hot tea.

Nathan turned down the car heater and opened the passenger side window to let some air in. The cool air on his face felt refreshing. Laughter and conversation from the group drifted across on the wind and Nathan got to work on his notes. It didn't take long before he understood what Fionn was talking about. Honest and confronting was one way of describing the debriefing conversation. Nathan didn't know how he'd react being part of a meeting such as this.

The Debrief

It's important to focus on positives, even the little ones.

S o, you know the routine, team. Left of the dealer,' Fionn said as he looked at Ciara. 'What went really well for you tonight from the moment you got the call?'

'Being ready for action really helped,' said Ciara. 'I was putting my daughter down for the night when the call came through. I was fortunate my sister, Olivia was there and she could take over. Based on the feedback from our last rescue I had my gear packed in anticipation of a call, so I was able to jump in the car straightaway. Thank you for that, by the way.' She looked around and made eye-contact with each of the team. 'I know I pushed back and made every excuse under the sun as to why I couldn't be as well prepared as everyone else, but that was rubbish. It was good feedback, thank you.'

Fionn clapped her on the back. 'Nice work, Ciara. And thanks for taking on the feedback. I'm delighted you put it into action.'

Fionn looked at Anna who was standing next to Ciara. 'Anna, you're up. What went well for you?'

Nathan zoned out a little as he concentrated on his notes. Each person shared what went well for them and they often referenced the feedback they received from the team that helped them not repeat the same mistakes. That was a neat idea, thought Nathan. He wondered how this might work for his own team.

'Thanks for sharing,' Fionn said to the group. 'I know some of you are still uncomfortable sharing what you did well, but it's important to recognise your own growth, and because the work we do is both physically and emotionally tough, it's important to focus on positives, even the little ones.' He paused for a moment to let his words sink in. 'Okay, round two. Ciara, what new lessons can we learn from what didn't go well?'

'For me, the big takeaway is to be more detailed in my route planning. I led us into a marsh, which when I relooked at the map, was an obvious feature I missed.'

Fionn nodded. 'Nice one,' he said. 'Anything else?'

Ciara thought for a moment. 'You were with me the whole time, did anything stand out for you?'

'Thanks for the opportunity to weigh in. I thought you did exceptionally well in taking the lead. There was one point on the walk when we ended up in unfamiliar terrain which could've been dangerous because we were walking blind for some of the walk. Maintaining that level of concentration is vital. You know, counting your steps, rechecking bearings and going again. It can be quite laborious but is essential on a night hike.'

Ciara nodded in agreement. 'Yeah, you're right. Thanks for reminding me.'

'All in all though, I thought you smashed it out there.'

Anna got a bit of slack over forgetting her gaiters and rain- proof trousers and gave Sophie, or Miss Perfect, some slack over her incessant use of checklists. They all laughed but Sophie smiled proudly.

'Hey!' she said jovially. 'I'm not the one with the wet trousers.'

'She's right about the checklists,' jumped in Ciara. I've started to use them myself. After our last rescue Sophie pulled me aside and explained that surgeons and pilots use them all the time. With so much going on in life and with so many things to remember under the pressure of urgency, checklists are great. I've even created a checklist to check against when I go travelling and even for packing my gear when I cycle into work. I can't count the amount of times I've forgotten my socks or underpants.'

'Whoa!' said Aisling. 'TMI TMI!' she said and then laughed.

'Okay, okay,' said Anna. 'I'll make a checklist when I get home.'

This conversation prompted Nathan to think about how he might be able to use checklists for himself. The work he does and the work the team does for that matter can be quite procedural, especially when it comes to software releases. This might be exactly what he needed as an additional quality-assurance tool. Too many things have been falling through the cracks; it was no one's fault, he recognised that the stress and pressure had a large part to play in it. However, if there was a checklist they could go back to, it might reduce slip-ups. He made a quick note.

The conversation had made its way back around to Fionn, and he was thinking about what could've been done better. Nathan thought Fionn did an exceptional job out there and listened with interest.

'Similar to Ciara, there was a time when I completely lost track of where we were on the map. I should've been paying more attention. Ciara was taking on the burden of navigation by herself and I know how tiring this can be. The concentration alone can be exhausting.'

Ciara jumped in. 'It wasn't your responsibility,' she said. 'I was the one responsible for the navigation.'

Fionn turned to Ciara. 'Thank you,' he said. 'Even though you were responsible for the navigation, I was accountable for the overarching rescue. I should've been paying more attention.'

Everyone nodded in agreement. 'Okay,' Fionn said energetically. 'Anything else that people noticed out there; something we might have missed?'

There was silence among the group. After a moment, Ciara spoke up. 'I think bringing Nathan along on the rescue was a mistake.'

Nathan could see, even at a distance, that Fionn bristled. 'How do you mean?' asked Fionn. 'Nathan is an experienced hillwalker. Granted he hasn't done it for a while, but we've been all over these mountains over the years.'

'I don't think that's the point.' It was Sophie speaking now.

'You put the rescue at risk by bringing a non-team member along.' There was agitation in Ciara's voice now. 'You were distracted the whole time and even though I wanted to lead the navigation, I could've done with some support. We might even have spotted Stephen much earlier, even on the way up if you weren't so distracted.'

'You have to remember that it was Nathan who spotted him in the end,' Fionn reminded them. It was clear from where Nathan was sitting that Fionn was starting to get defensive. Nathan was pretty pissed off at Ciara's comments. Wasn't he the hero of the moment?

'Fionn, he tore off as soon as he saw a glimpse of Stephen's headlamp. It was awesome that he spotted him, but what if he'd broken his ankle charging off in the dark like that. We'd have been rescuing two people off the mountain tonight. Even though it was a successful rescue I think we were more lucky than professional tonight,' said Ciara.

'She's right, Fionn,' said Sophie.

Fionn looked around at the faces of the rest of the team. They were all nodding in agreement. Begrudgingly, Fionn agreed. As angry as Nathan was for not being recognised for his part, he also saw the truth of it.

'You're right,' Fionn finally said before he turned to Ciara. 'Thank you. I appreciate you raising that and calling it out. It was a risk to the rescue and I should have been more cognizant of that.'

Ciara nodded. Clearly, she felt uncomfortable calling out the team leader.

'Perhaps you could add it to your checklist,' said Sienna as seriously as she could. Everyone laughed.

'Ha! Ha! Ha!' Sophie said sarcastically before she began to laugh.

The last question Fionn asked of the team was, 'Based on what we learnt, how can we improve our processes to consistently achieve excellence?' But Nathan had stopped listening.

The Democrat

They're different from negative critiques because they focus on learning from experience.

W hat's up? How's the knee?'

Fionn drove through the darkness. The narrow road was lit up only fifty or so metres ahead of them.

'Nothing really, just tired,' Nathan replied.

'I'm not surprised. You must still be jet-lagged from arriving only a few days ago.'

'What an arsehole!' Nathan blurted out.

'Who? What do you mean?'

'Ciara! I'm the one who spotted Stephen. He could still be lying out there if it wasn't for me. Who the hell is she to say that I shouldn't have come along on the rescue?' Nathan was furious.

'So you heard that, huh?'

'Yeah, I heard it. How the hell could you take it? How old is she, twelve!'

Fionn couldn't help but laugh.

'How could you take that kinda criticism? Isn't she new to this and here she is telling you that you were wrong. And you took it!'

'Okay! Okay!' said Fionn as he tried to calm things down. 'Clearly you're upset.' Fionn paused. 'She was right. I didn't like it that she was right, but she was. You're not trained in mountain rescue. If anything had happened to you out there we'd have been screwed. An investigation would have ensued and I'd probably get my arse handed to me.'

'Okay, so maybe she had a point, but she's got some balls calling out a superior like that.'

Fionn was silent for a moment. 'That's not how we operate as a team. Each person has different responsibilities; mine just happens to be team leader. It doesn't mean I get a pass when I mess up. If you don't mind me saying so, that's your ego talking. Anyone in the team should be able to call anyone else out. Not in a mean way, but they should be able to point out when they've done something wrong, so it can be corrected and not repeated.'

Nathan was quiet. Fionn let him mull over his thoughts for a while until eventually he picked up the conversation.

'Look, we always debrief after a rescue, whether we're successful or not. That way we keep improving and we don't make the same mistakes; new mistakes, sure. But not the same ones. It's based on the same model used by the Navy Seals.'

This grabbed Nathan's attention so Fionn continued.

'The Navy SEALs have a powerful three-question method to learn from any event to boost performance. Imagine the power of analysing projects or important tasks in a way that goes beyond just pointing out mistakes; that's the power of After-Action Reviews (AARs). They're different from negative critiques because they focus on learning from experience. I use them with the team on every rescue or training session and I use them with my teams at work. Here's how they work:

1. **Celebrate Wins:** We start by asking, 'What new, positive things did we learn from what went well?' Our brains tend to dwell on negatives, so it's crucial to highlight successes we can build on.

2. **Turn Challenges into Lessons:** After celebrating wins, we move to constructive feedback. But instead of simply asking 'What went wrong?' We ask, 'What new lessons can we learn from what didn't go well?' This approach focuses on future improvement.

3. **Setting the Standard for Excellence:** Once we've learnt from both successes and challenges, we look ahead. We combine the insights from the first two steps and ask, 'Based on what we learnt, how can we improve our processes to consistently achieve excellence?' This reinforces the idea that excellence is the goal, and clear processes are the tools to get there.

'Those debriefs are a huge part of the Democratic Leadership Style.' Fionn glanced at Nathan who was still in a sulk, so he decided to keep on talking with the hope of loosening him up.

'The purpose of the Democratic Leadership Style is to ensure that everyone has a voice. Everyone, regardless of their position in the team, feels heard. This way, everyone is likely to buy into a decision, even if they don't fully agree with it initially. Of course, not every team conversation is going to be fun and laughter, we have to discuss the difficult things too.

Those debriefs can be uncomfortable, but everyone knows it's a safe space to debate the issues; ego is left at the metaphorical door.'

At this point, Nathan smiled, so Fionn continued.

'Some of the traits of the Democratic Leader are obvious but one of the standouts is they're very good at managing conflict, both when they're involved and when mediating for others.

'Of course, one of the downsides is that they can be slow to make a decision and people can get frustrated. They might feel that everyone should have a voice and they go round and round in circles wasting precious time. You'll rarely find a Democratic Leader in a start-up, especially when time to market is an important commercial advantage. They just wouldn't last.'

Nathan was nodding as his thumbs worked the digital keyboard on his iPhone. Fionn knew that asking questions at this late hour probably wasn't the right thing to do, so he kept going with his thoughts on the Democratic Leadership Style.

'The other thing to be mindful of, is if the leader's team is relatively young or inexperienced, then it's best not to leave a decision open to them. It can be demoralising to be asked for your viewpoint and then have it seemingly ignored. It's best to discuss any decisions with them openly and encourage questions for understanding until they're at the level where they can provide meaningful input.'

'So going back to that delegation model you talked about earlier.'

'What was that?' Fionn was caught up in his stream of consciousness and wasn't expecting Nathan to interject.

'You know, the delegation model you talked about. It's about gradually giving a person more and more responsibility for their tasks until you can hand them over completely because they now know as much as or more than you.'

'Yeah, that's right,' said Fionn, delighted Nathan was lifting from his dark mood. 'Just to reiterate, an important part of the Democratic Leadership Style is to ensure that everyone, regardless of their position in the team, has a voice. Once you give it to them you can't take it away, even, or especially, when you don't like what they say. If someone is upset about something I genuinely want to hear about it because now we can have a conversation about it, and hopefully, resolve it. That's the purpose of those debriefing sessions. Everyone is expected to contribute for the greater good of the team. For me, it's less about what people say, it's more about how they're saying it. Sometimes people can be rude or aggressive in their delivery, which goes against our team norms, and the style of delivery is addressed, but we talk openly about the content.'

Nathan was mulling this over and Fionn knew he was wrestling with how his ego would take such a challenge.

'So, if you think about it, you'd never use the Democratic Leadership Style in an emergency; that's where the commanding and even pace-setting styles come to the fore and once the goal has been achieved we back off from those styles.'

Nathan nodded. He flicked his finger up the iPhone screen until he got to his notes on the Commanding Style and Pace-Setter Style and shared these with Fionn to ensure he'd captured the salient points.

'Nice work,' said Fionn. 'One other important thing to remember about the Pace-Setter Style is that it is often synonymous with the Peter Principle.' Fionn paused to see if Nathan recognised this term. He continued to tap away at his keyboard so Fionn continued.

'The Peter Principle is defined as "People rise to the level of their own incompetence". For example, let's say you've got a software developer named Peter, and he can cut code like nobody's business. He smashes it out and it's good quality too. He's clearly exceptional. The company recognises this and they say, 'We've got to hang onto this guy, what should we do? Well, how about we promote him to lead the software development team?' And so they do.

'Now, if Peter's lucky he has a team of like-minded pace-setters who thrive in smashing out code. If they have a question, they can go to Peter, he can give them the answer and they can continue producing high-quality, high-volume work. So now, the company recognises Peter's exceptional ability to lead a team and they say, 'We've got to hang onto this guy, what should we do? Well, how about we promote him to lead the whole production team?' And so they do. And now Peter is responsible for the oversight of the software development team, the architecture team, the test analysis team, the business analysis team and the project management team.' Fionn paused to let this sink in. 'Can you see any impending problems here?'

Nathan thought about it for a moment. 'Well, yeah sure. The architects and analysts are less likely to operate at a pace-setter's speed because of the very nature of their work — analysis. They're likely to want time to think things through, and besides, if they come to Peter about a problem related to their field, Peter might not be able to help them because he's not an expert in those disciplines.'

'That's right!' said Fionn. 'So what's likely to happen?'

'What's likely to happen is that Peter will get extremely stressed and impatient. He'll probably blame the team for not performing the way he'd expect them to and go home and kick the cat. He'd probably blame any poor team performance on the fact that he inherited a bunch of losers.' Nathan was building momentum and thoughts flowed out of him. 'But Peter would be trapped because with each promotion comes more money, which he has used to buy a bigger house and a new car. He has shaped his lifestyle around his new level of income.' Fionn went silent and waited for the realisation to land.

'I guess that's the position I find myself in,' Nathan said solemnly. 'You know, Fiona and I have recently moved to a larger property and upgraded our cars. I guess I feel trapped like our friend, Peter.'

'So what are Peter's options?' asked Fionn quietly.

'Well, I guess he could continue in his role and be miserable.'

'Ha! Ha! That's one option. What else?'

Nathan smiled to himself as he recognised that powerful coaching question. 'Hmmm … he could go back to his previous role where he felt productive and was happier, but that would be a real kick in the ego, and besides, it might mean less money. Could he risk that?'

Fionn nodded as Nathan reasoned his way through his options.

'He could leave the company and look for an equal-sized role somewhere else in the hope that things might be better there.' Nathan paused. 'But that doesn't address the underlying issue, does it? He might bring his misery with him and spread it around a different team.' Nathan paused to think some more and Fionn waited, confident that Nathan would land on the solution; the only viable solution. He wasn't disappointed.

'I suppose what Peter ultimately has to do if he wants to be successful in his career at that level is learn to be a people leader instead of a technical leader.'

'That's it!' Fionn's enthusiasm startled Nathan and caused him to smile. 'One of the problems with the Pace-Setter Leader is they tend to rely on old skills and lack the awareness of new skills necessary to be successful at higher levels of leadership. They lack the cooperation needed for real leadership. Don't get me wrong,' said Fionn. 'It's entirely acceptable for

Peter to remain a technical leader if that's his preference. He is, after all, playing to his strengths and if he's comfortable there, fantastic. However, if he wants to rise through the ranks of an organisation he will have to learn a whole new set of skills and you nailed it when you said he would have to learn how to become a people leader.'

Nathan nodded in agreement, so Fionn continued.

'When people come to me asking what they need to do to get to the next level in their career I tell them to climb back down the rungs of the career ladder that they've been climbing to date, pick up their ladder and move it to a different wall and start at the bottom rung. Leadership skills are very different from technical skills. In fact, even how we learn leadership skills is very different from *how* we learn technical skills.

'Remember how we talked earlier about how leadership skills are developed and stored in limbic system?'

Nathan hesitated. 'You'll have to give it to me again,' he said.

'Well, when it comes to learning technical skills, we use the part of the brain known collectively as the neocortex; it's colloquially referred to as the "thinking brain". Leadership skills, like all soft skills such as communication, emotional regulation, managing stress, and so on, are developed and stored in the limbic system or the "emotional brain". And this difference is massive.' Fionn paused to let the importance of what he'd said settle.

'The difference comes down to how these parts of the brain learn. The neocortex is a very rapid learner; it can learn things such as risk management or accounting principles quite quickly; however, the limbic system is a much slower learner. It's a much slower learner not because it's trying to learn something new, it's a much slower learner because it's trying to learn something new on top of already deeply ingrained habits.

'Let's take communication as an example. We've been communicating and learning to communicate from the day we're born. Now, if how we're communicating isn't working for us it might be time to learn new communication skills, but here's the problem. It's practically impossible to communicate at a conscious level; there's too much complexity, not only in the English language, but in any language. You have nouns and verbs, adnouns, adverbs, adjectives and also sentence structures and the different meanings of words. If we had to think about everything we had to say consciously we'd never get a word out.' Fionn paused. 'Does that make sense so far?'

'I think so,' said Nathan hesitantly.

'What I mean is that if we communicate unconsciously we've got to be able to consciously interrupt the patterns that aren't working and relearn new patterns so they become the dominant unconscious responses. The same is true for leadership skills. We talked earlier about how we learn leadership skills, remember? We model it from others and this is very much an unconscious process; therefore, if we want to change our leadership style we've got to approach the learning in a different way.

'In order for the limbic system to learn, it requires lots of practice and lots of repetition. Lots of practice and lots of repetition.'

Nathan was nodding as his thumbs worked frantically to record his notes.

'Lots of practice and lots of repetition,' Fionn repeated.

Nathan laughed. 'I get it. I get it. I get it.'

'Seriously though, this is important to understand because leadership is hard. There are a lot of demands, not only on a leader's time, but also on their cognitive load. It can be a very stressful position and we—'

Nathan jumped in to finish Fionn's sentence. 'We always go back to what we know under times of stress.'

Fionn laughed. 'Right again. But here's why it's so important that we practise leadership skills to the point where they occur unconsciously or are habitual. If we're tasked with juggling a lot of balls in the air at the same time, while trying to solve complex problems, and deal with other challenges going on at the same time, the cognitive load can be huge. This is when the cracks start to form and our ability to regulate our emotions becomes a challenge. However, if our leadership skills and communication skills, etc. are habitual the brain uses so much less energy, which can be diverted to dealing with the challenges, that we are facing in the moment.'

'That makes a lot of sense,' Nathan said thoughtfully. When Nathan looked up from his notes he noticed that they were back in civilization. Music leaked from the bars along the streets and couples stumbled along the pathway laughing and joking as they went. Nathan yawned loudly and looked at the clock on the car dashboard; it was 2.04 a.m. Fionn seemed wide awake and as alert as ever.

Nathan was finishing up his notes when he remembered the team joking about checklists. He mentioned it to Fionn.

Fionn laughed at the memory. 'Yeah, it's something that Sophie has been on about for ages. She uses them religiously and the team has started to pick up on them and use them more and more. I use them myself. How do you think I was so confident we could just jump in the car at a moment's notice and know everything we needed was packed and in its rightful place? The answer is, *the simple checklist.* The problem we have is that our knowledge and the world's complexity are growing and making it harder to remember everything crucial in high-stakes situations. Even experts can overlook simple but critical steps, so the simplest solution is to have checklists. They ensure essential steps aren't missed, even by experts.

'Checklists tend to come in two forms: "Do-Confirm" which means pause and confirm completion of memorised steps, and "Read-Do" which means complete tasks as you check them off. Simple, right?' said Fionn.

'Sophie is always reminding us that checklists have saved lives in medicine, improved aviation safety, and how they can be applied in many different fields. They can also promote teamwork and communication by ensuring everyone's on the same page about critical steps. Why most people laugh about them and resist is that they can feel bureaucratic or insulting to experts. However, Sophie has convinced me that they are tools to support, not replace, expertise. To be effective the simple checklist needs to be clear, concise, and focused on essential steps.'

'I like it,' said Nathan. 'I'm going to see how I can use these with my own team. In fact, having a simple checklist for my recent flight would've helped. I had to waste a hundred euro on a new pair of shoes for the funeral because I forgot to pack them in the rush.'

Fionn laughed and pulled the car into the driveway.

The Order

Remember M.E.C.E.?

The clock on the old video cassette player showed it was just before 3 a.m. Nathan sat on the old sofa in the same room where he had spent many a night, sharing stories and laughter in years gone by. In some ways it seemed as if it was only yesterday, but in others it seemed as though it was a whole other life. He was feeling much more comfortable now that was in his "travel clothes" as he called them. Black combat trousers with loads of pockets for his ticket and passport and wallet and all the small essentials for travel and a black long-sleeved T-shirt. His bright orange crocs were next to his suitcase ready for action when it was time to leave for the airport. Nathan checked the time again, two hours and fifty-four minutes to go. One of his legs was elevated and his trouser leg pulled down. He tied an ice-pack to the side of his knee to reduce the swelling. The pain wasn't too bad but carrying his luggage from the rented car reminded him it was still there. The last thing he wanted to do was travel for thirty-six hours with an angry knee.

Fionn made his way carefully into the room holding two cups of coffee.

'Are you sure you want to stay up all night?' Nathan asked Fionn. 'I don't mind watching a movie.'

'Not at all,' said Fionn as he placed one of the coffees on a side table next to Nathan.

'There are a lot of memories in this room, aren't there?' said Nathan.

'Sure are!' Fionn replied with a chuckle.

'I don't want to seem like a bore, but I've really learnt a lot from you tonight. There's a part of me that wants to gain as much of your knowledge about leadership as I can while I have the opportunity. You see, what's really frustrating is I've read a lot about leadership and it's great in theory, but I guess what I've been missing is how to translate it into practice.'

'I don't think you're alone there. Having a coach really helped accelerate my growth and I couldn't see myself without one. I've found that just having someone to talk through things with has been a real godsend. You have to do the work yourself, of course, but you don't have to do it alone.'

'We've only got a couple of hours, but if it's okay with you, can I pick your brains some more?' asked Nathan.

'Pick away,' said Fionn. 'There's nothing like a bit of brain picking with a half-naked man sitting on my sofa.'

'Hey,' Nathan looked down. 'A quarter-naked!'

Fionn snorted in his coffee and wiped a small spill from his trousers.

'So we've worked our way through the six leadership styles and I loved that I was able to see them all in action in a single night. But that's out there on the mountains, the office environment is a little different, isn't it?' said Nathan.

'Of course, but the principles are the same. Leading a team is leading a team. The context may change but human nature, not so much. Let's talk about your situation at work. You said that your team hates you, they don't work well together and collectively aren't performing, but they still enjoy having a bit of banter and heading out for a coffee once in a while.'

'Well, I didn't say all of that, but it's pretty accurate. There are so many rookie mistakes, they're not really a team, none of them take responsibility for anything and they keep going over my head to Claudia. It's as frustrating as all hell!' Nathan was getting agitated and took a sip of his coffee.

'Okay,' said Fionn. Based on the six leadership styles that we talked about tonight, if you imagine each one represents a lever. All the levers are on to some degree or another depending on what's happening at a particular time; however, in your situation where your team isn't performing, which of the leadership styles do you think you should be leading with? Which of the levers should you be pulling on the hardest at this time?'

'That's easy,' replied Nathan without even needing to think about it. 'It's the Visionary Leadership Style. That's the most positively impactful, right? So for bang for buck it seems like using this style will give me a quick win.'

'Hmmm … it's not the one I'd lead out on. Now, of course, context matters and with your context in mind, how much buy-in do you think you'd get from the team if you went to them and said, 'Okay, everyone! We're going to set a team vision.''

Nathan imagined the scenario in his head and it didn't look good.

'Look, I know you're tired and I know you want as much information as you can take back with you, so how about I just share my thoughts.'

'That would be great,' said Nathan looking decidedly relieved.

'If I were in your shoes, or even if I was just building a team from scratch, I'd always start with the Affiliative Leadership Style. It's absolutely essential that you build trust with the individuals in your team and at your peer level. Remember M.E.C.E.? We'll get back to that. Without trust, people will do what you ask, but they'll do it because of your position, your authority, not because of you. People don't follow titles, they follow people they trust.'

'Okay, that makes sense,' said Nathan.

'Next, I'd pull hard on the Coaching Leadership Style lever. Now, that's not to say I'd take my hand off the Affiliative Style, that's always going to be on to some degree. However, after building some form of relationship with them I want to demonstrate that I'm interested in helping them grow and succeed in their careers. To do this I'd spend time with them working through some of their challenges and looking for opportunities to help them grow in the direction that they want to take their careers.' Fionn paused for a moment before continuing. 'I remember I was leading a project a few years ago and on my team was a wonderful woman named Bonnie. She was part of the customer support team and she was fantastic with customers, and after a couple of conversations, it became clear that she wanted to become a trainer. So, I immediately gave her the responsibility for developing the training materials we needed for project go-live and to be the person to lead the training sessions when the time came.

'She was nervous but delighted. The project was about eighteen months away from completion, so I began to guide her on what she needed to do to get started and guess what tool I used to do that?'

'Would that be the G.R.O.W. model per chance?' Nathan said with a laugh.

'It would indeed.' Fionn laughed. 'So, even though it took Bonnie much longer to pull everything together to an acceptable quality it didn't matter, we had the time. She even went off and did some personal study in the evening and became a certified trainer for adult learners.'

'Wow, that's awesome,' said Nathan. 'What's she doing now?'

'I'm not sure. We haven't been in touch in quite some time, but after my project she was picked up by another project manager and asked to lead the training component of that project.

'Not all professional development needs to occur through coaching conversations though. It's just as easy to buy a book for someone in the area that they're interested in, or look for secondments in another team, or even help them find a mentor in the area in which they want to grow. It's a matter of demonstrating that you are completely invested in them and in their careers.'

'I see,' said Nathan. 'Sounds good. So the next lever you'd pull would be the Visionary one, right?'

'Not yet, my friend,' said Fionn.

Nathan looked a little confused and Fionn could see he was trying to analyse each of the remaining styles. 'The next one is the Democratic Leadership Style.'

Nathan looked perplexed.

'Think about it for a moment,' said Fionn. 'What would happen if you brought everyone together and asked them to look to the future when it's quite possible they're still carrying some baggage from the past — things they haven't been able to let go of just yet?'

'I guess they'll keep bringing up reasons why they can't move forward and keep bringing up all the unresolved issues.'

'That's right,' said Fionn. 'That's exactly what tends to happen. So we've got to give them an opportunity to get everything out of their system in a safe, non-judgement, environment.'

'An environment of—' Nathan swiped through the notes on his phone. 'Unconditional positive regard.'

Fionn couldn't help but laugh.

'So how do you do that,' asked Nathan.

'It's actually easier than you might think. Firstly, organise a two-hour team meeting. Hand out Post-it notes and ask this question: What are some of the challenges that we as a team are facing? Give everyone a few minutes to write things out and you do the same. Encourage them to get everything out, give them examples of some of the trickier things that should be raised but they might be afraid to talk about. You could say, 'What about the arsehole of a boss you've been lumped with? Somebody get that down. What about the unreasonable demands around timelines from senior management? Somebody capture that one.' And so on.

'Once everyone has jotted down a few thoughts and ideas, ask them to put them up on the board. Before the last two people sit down, ask them to group the ideas into themes and give the themes a name. It's important that the team is fully involved in this activity, your job is to facilitate and guide.'

Nathan was jotting everything down in a small notebook he always brought with him when travelling.

'Now, here's the crucial point. Even if somebody puts down something that challenges your authority.' Fionn shivered at the word. 'Or writes something that is painful to hear, you must not make a big deal of it. If you do, you will lose the team. They will never open up again. Never. In fact, if you turn around and thank the person for putting it down and commend them on their honesty or courage or whatever comes to mind, you'll send the signal that people can say anything and it's okay; they won't be punished for it. Open and honest conversations are allowed in this team. Do that and it will change the whole dynamic.'

Nathan imagined himself in this scenario. He thought that although it might be tough he could see the benefits to it.

'So now, once you go through each of the themes and take the time to review them in detail, as well as ask the team to elaborate, so they feel like they've had a chance to talk them through we ask, 'So, which one of these themes, as a team, are we going to tackle first?''

Nathan was scribbling away, so Fionn paused to allow him to catch up.

'Once they select one of the themes you ask, 'What would good look like in this situation?''

Nathan smiled. 'You're using the G.R.O.W. model? He said, delighted with himself.

'That's exactly right! So once they've analysed the "Reality", defined the "Goal", next we move onto the "Options" and "Obstacles", and finally the "Way Forward".'

'That's really clever. I like it,' said Nathan.

'Why thank you very much,' Fionn replied. 'You'll be surprised how the team starts jumping in with ideas and solutions. It works like a charm.'

The two friends each sipped their coffee. Fionn yawned and shook his head to shake off the tiredness. Nathan didn't feel tired at all; in fact, he felt energised and full of ideas for when he got back.

'So, of course, the next Leadership Style we go to is the Visionary Leadership Style. Only when we've drained the swamp can we consider moving forward, and in reality, if the team is already coming up with options for solving some of the issues they raised, the next step is relatively straight forward.'

'What's that then?' asked Nathan.

'We ask: How do we, as a team, want to be recognised by the rest of the organisation? What do we want to be known for? What's our purpose as a team? What's our vision?'

'I like the way you put it like that. It's a much better way of jumping straight into the ol' 'Let's do a team vision, everyone.'' Nathan waved his arms stiffly like a puppet. 'Sometimes these things sound so dry and staged, but I like this framework. It comes from a solid foundation of improving things and moving forward.'

'Thank you,' said Fionn as he swirled his coffee round the cup before finishing it off. 'Okay, let's wrap up the Leadership Style levers.'

Nathan nodded.

'Once this is set up it's time for you to take a step back and let the team lead itself. You don't become completely hands-off, but your role is to clear the way of any obstacles and help the team work through problems and challenges. With this foundation in place you can become a servant leader, one who serves your team and lets them lead. Trying to do this without having this foundation in place would be a disaster. All you have to do now is ensure that everyone continues to meet the team objectives and if their behaviour drops below expectations you have a conversation with them about it.'

'Oh yeah,' said Nathan, suddenly remembering. 'We need to talk about feedback. Especially feedback for millennials.'

'No problem. Before we do, it's important to know that every now and again it will be required for the team to pick up their pace in order to hit an important milestone. You'll have to move into the Pace-Setter Style, but it doesn't have to be in a harsh, crack the whip kind of way. You can explain the situation to the team and ask them how they think everyone can solve it. There might be a bit of moaning and groaning and again, once they feel heard and understood, we encourage them to move into problem-solving mode. Your job is to remove as many obstacles as you can, buy the pizza, rub their backs, and stay out of their way.'

Nathan smiled to himself as he enjoyed a moment imagining himself as that type of leader, and even though it was only in his imagination, he felt a brief moment of pride.

'Using the Commanding Leadership Style is something I try to stay away from; however, it can be useful if you've got someone on your team who is not performing. When you've tried everything else, building the trust, coaching, feedback, and so on and nothing is working you can become quite commanding in your nature. Not in a harsh way but in a very direct way. Tell them exactly what you want them to do and when you want it to be completed. You'll be surprised, sometimes all they're looking for is clear direction and expectations. They haven't learnt to take the initiative yet. This, of course, would form the basis of your coaching conversations; to help them build the confidence in themselves or just to help get a better understanding of what's preventing them from taking ownership, or whatever the issue is. You might be surprised how effective it can be.

'So to recap, we start off with the Affiliative Leadership Style followed by the Coaching Leadership Style. These two styles focus on the individual. Next we bring the team together and build that trust within the team by using the Democratic Leadership Style, which is closely followed by the Visionary Leadership Style. So go from individual focus to team focus. Easy right?'

Nathan laughed as he faked nervousness.

'Have you ever come across the expression: Steel fist wrapped in a velvet glove?' asked Fionn.

'Yeah,' said Nathan. 'It makes me think I can't trust the person. You know, that they're just being nice on the outside, but on the inside they're really a tyrant.'

'I know what you mean. I've never liked the expression, but sometimes it's necessary to bring a little steel to a conversation; not every message is going to be a positive one for an individual or even the team as a whole and when we deliver it we can't fluff around the edges, we have to be clear and concise. Not mean or nasty, but clear and concise.'

'So can you give me an example of a *steel* conversation?' asked Nathan.

'A steel conversation would be one around addressing poor performance, or if the organisation is going through change and tough decisions have to be made. Being clear in these situations is being kind.'

Nathan nodded his agreement.

'The way I like to think about it is that the Visionary, Coaching, Affiliative and Democratic Styles all fall under the velvet category, and when we introduce the Pace-Setter and Commanding Styles, we're bringing in the steel. So what are your thoughts about how to bring the steel in an appropriate and professional manner? They tend to be tough conversations after all.'

Nathan thought for a moment, but other than being overly direct and unsympathetic, which he knew wasn't the answer, he drew a blank. He shook his head. 'I can't think of anything,' he said.

'The answer lies in our values, our values as a team, our values as an organisation. As long as we deliver the message with our values in mind, as long as we deliver the message wrapped in our values, we will always deliver the message in a professional way.'

Nathan nodded as he scribbled down these last few points.

'I need a top-up,' said Fionn suddenly. 'Can I get you one?'

'Yes, please,' said Nathan as he handed Fionn his empty cup.

The break gave Nathan a chance to review his notes and pull out the salient points.

The Most Important Thing

It's a model I adhere to closely and it works really well.

Nathan closed his eyes for a short moment. He was looking forward to being able to sleep on the plane. The big struggle would be queueing up to board his flight. The delays in Dublin Airport have become legendary since Covid with people overeager to catch up on their international holidays and the airport being short of staff. He would have plenty of time though, and he was more or less packed. All he had to do was to throw his suitcase into the back of the car and he was away. At this hour of the morning there wouldn't be much traffic at all and Blanchardstown wasn't too far from the airport anyway.

He heard the door click closed and he opened his eyes. Fionn placed his cup of coffee next to him on the side table as Nathan scanned his notes.

'You place a lot of emphasis on building trust,' said Nathan.

'Absolutely!' said Fionn. As tired as he was, Nathan could clearly see Fionn's enthusiasm for the subject matter.

'When I said earlier that without trust there can be nothing else?'

Nathan nodded.

'I really meant it. Several years ago a team of researchers at Google set out to discover what made a high-performing team. Interestingly enough, it didn't come down to the make up of the team itself, it came down to these five key dynamics: **Psychological Safety**, **Dependability**, **Structure and Clarity**, **Meaning**, and **Impact**.'

Nathan didn't look up from his notes as he frantically jotted these points down.

'Let me talk about them individually,' said Fionn.

Nathan nodded, still concentrating on his notes, so Fionn continued.

'The first one, and by far the most important factor according to the study, is psychological safety. It means team members feel safe to take risks, admit mistakes, and be vulnerable without fear of being judged or punished. What it doesn't mean is that leaders aren't allowed to have difficult conversations or be held to account for poor performance. It has been twisted over the years by people who might feel a little uncomfortable about being asked to do something, even if that something is well within their job description, they pull out the 'I don't feel psychologically safe card'. I normally listen and recognise what they might be feeling and then explain that is not what it means. I then go on to explain what it does mean and continue the conversation as before.' Fionn paused and listened to the scratching of Nathan's pen in his notebook in the otherwise quiet of the early morning. After a moment, he continued.

'Dependability is the next one and it comes down to team members being able to rely on each other to follow through on commitments and deliver high-quality work.

'Structure and clarity is next, which comes down to having clear goals, roles, and plans for how the work will get done. Everyone understands their part and how it contributes to the bigger picture.

'The fourth key dynamic of a team is meaning, in which all team members feel their work is important and has a positive impact. This very much aligns to the team vision we talked about earlier. Being able to answer the question: Why do we exist? Why are we a team?' Again Fionn paused to allow Nathan to catch up before continuing.

'Lastly, we have impact. This is all about the team having a clear sense of the impact of their work and how it contributes to the success of the organisation.

'In summary, these findings have important implications for how teams are built and managed. By focusing on creating a psychologically safe environment, setting clear goals, and fostering a sense of meaning and impact, organisations can increase the likelihood of their teams reaching their full potential. It's a model I adhere to closely and it works really well.' Fionn looked out of the window of the small room; the curtains were open and his eyes were drawn to the street lamp outside. Drizzle coated the window and he relished the warmth of the room after being cold for most of the night. When the sound of Nathan capturing his notes ceased, he looked at his friend.

Nathan ran his pen down the pages of notes to ensure he understood everything Fionn had shared. He nodded a couple of times before looking up.

'This is great,' he said. 'In theory! But how do you actually go about doing this stuff?'

'Well, some of it is obvious, right? Creating structure and clarity just takes a little time to define roles, get clear on goals and ensure the team has a plan to achieve these. Impact is aligning this work to the goals or strategy of the organisation, and meaning is helping the team build their vision. The first two, psychological safety and dependability are trickier. These take time and ...' Fionn purposely trailed off.

'Vulnerability trust?' said Nathan.

'Awesome! That's exactly right. Easier said than done; I'll grant you that. So let's talk about Lencioni's work.'

'Oh yeah, you mentioned him before.'

'I sure did,' said Fionn as he sat up in his chair, clearly getting into another gear. 'I use a lot of Lencioni's work in building my teams. Lencioni is a management consultant and he's been around for quite a while. During his time studying teams, he recognised that when teams aren't performing well, if you go back in time about six to eight months there is always a seed subtly planted, which over time, turns into a weed that chokes a blossoming team.'

Nathan couldn't help but smile at the rather weak analogy.

'Really?' he asked. 'Is that the best you can come up with?' He laughed.

'It's 4 a.m. in the morning, dude. What do you want from me? he said and laughed. 'Okay, you get the point though, right? That seed always tends to be a lack of trust that works its way into the team, and more specifically, the absence of vulnerability trust which causes people to stay in their lanes and not put their heads above the parapet for fear of being called out or embarrassed about sharing an idea that goes against the traditional thinking of the team.' Fionn could see Nathan frantically scribbling in his notebook.

'Here, let's do it this way. Draw a large triangle on a new page and divide it into five layers. The bottom layer is Vulnerability Trust and we've talked about this extensively, but basically when there is no vulnerability there is only invulnerability. The sense that 'I don't make mistakes' and 'Mistakes aren't tolerated here'. This kind of messaging leads the team to adopt the same mindset; therefore, when mistakes are made they will more than likely try and shove them under the carpet to avoid blame or to point the finger at someone or something else as the cause, because in their minds, they fear punishment or retribution. This kind of environment strangles innovation and it prevents any kind of healthy conflict and healthy conflict is essential for any team to grow.' Fionn closed his eyes for a moment and listened to the quiet of the early morning. After a moment he continued.

'So, without trust there is a fear of conflict. The problem here is that if a team is reluctant to engage in conflict, to rigorously debate the important issues, the loudest and most dominant voice tends to win out and that's not a team, it's one person drowning out the collective knowledge of the team. It's also extremely unhealthy from a team relationship point of view because without conflict we end up with a *false harmony*.'

Nathan looked up from his notes. It was a term he hadn't heard before, but he sensed it was an important concept.

'False harmony occurs when a group appears agreeable on the surface but lacks true consensus or open communication. It's basically going along to get along, even if there are underlying disagreements or reservations. People avoid expressing dissenting opinions, even if they have them, for fear of conflict or rocking the boat or there tends to be a greater focus on politeness over candour; you know, discussions may be overly polite and lack the kind of frank exchange of ideas that can lead to better solutions. Other examples of false harmony that I've seen are the unwillingness to address problems, so difficult issues are swept under the rug, which can lead to problems festering and resurfacing later. Ultimately, false harmony can be detrimental to teams and organisations because it stifles creativity, hinders problem-solving, and can lead to poor decision-making.

'This is why it's so important for a team to engage in healthy conflict, and just to stress the point, this can't occur fully without an environment of vulnerability trust because I have to know that you're not attacking me personally, you're challenging my idea because you genuinely believe that it's wrong or not yet fully formed. This way, the best ideas bubble up to the surface.'

'So this is where the skills of the Democratic Leader come into play; to facilitate these discussions,' added Nathan.

'Exactly,' said Fionn as he yawned and rubbed his eyes.

Nathan pushed down the feelings of guilt he felt for keeping Fionn up through the night, but he was enjoying this time with his friend and knew he wouldn't see him again for a long time.

'It's important to remember though, it's not a case of gloves off and no rules. My guiding principle is to never cross the line into what Lencioni refers to as "mean-spirited personal attacks" where the person is attacked, not the idea. It's best to think of conflict as sitting on a continuum; at one end you have "false harmony" and at the other is "mean-spirited personal attacks". On this continuum there is a half-way point, never cross it,' said Fionn. 'That way we can have robust debates and people can contribute their thoughts and views without the fear of being ridiculed or shut down.'

Nathan finished his notes and tapped the end of his pen against the notebook. 'But what about team differences or even cultural differences; doesn't this come into it? I mean if you were in Italy, and I know I'm stereotyping here, the conversations are likely to be more robust and fierier, right? Compared to, again, I'm stereotyping, a team in Japan; which is more likely to be more controlled and subdued. Which approach is right?'

'That's an awesome question and the answer is, it depends. It depends on what's right for the team. It's always a good idea to discuss with your team how you're going to engage in conflict; a manifesto, if you will. It could sound something like, 'We, the members of this team, recognize that conflict is an inevitable and even valuable part of a high-performing team. We commit to embracing healthy conflict as a catalyst for growth, innovation, and achieving our shared goals.''

'Wow! That's pretty good, can you give that to me again?' asked Nathan.

Fionn repeated it. 'This is just an example of what one could sound like, it's important that you develop it with your team to gain buy-in into the idea. What's also important is to create a few values as part of the manifesto that act as guidelines.'

'Hmmm,' said Nathan, nodding his head. 'I can see where this would be useful. Kinda like ground rules for how we engage some of the thornier issues.'

Fionn glanced at the clock. 'Okay, so, without conflict there is a lack of commitment; that's the next level. And without conflict you end up with ambiguity and uncertainty and frustration within the team. Let's say, for example, a few of us from the team are travelling to an important meeting, and because of budget cuts, we're told by Human Resources, that when we travel, we have to fly economy instead of business class.'

'Sounds like a timely example.' Nathan laughed.

Fionn laughed too and continued. 'So we meet at the terminal and we're chatting about the trip and the importance of the upcoming meeting and we're called to board. I check in through the express lane and although you all think this is a little unusual you brush it off as me being a little cheeky, until, that is, you see me sitting comfortably in business class with a pre-flight drink in my hand. I smile and raise my glass.

'You are completely confused. 'Hey, I thought we were all supposed to be travelling economy, remember? Our head of HR specifically told us this,' you say. Clearly you're frustrated, but I simply smile. 'Oh no, that didn't mean me. I'm leading the negotiations so I need to be fresh and ready to go when we land. Enjoy your flight,' I say. What do you think everyone is thinking?'

'Everyone will be fuming. I can imagine a good dose of "healthy conflict" coming your way.'

'And deservedly so. Without clear commitment there is likely to be ambiguity and with ambiguity the team can start to fall apart because it's difficult to hold people to account for their decisions and actions. That's an extreme example and it may sound strange but people tend to buy into ideas less if they don't feel they've been able to contribute, when they don't feel they've been heard. Conversely, when people do feel heard, genuinely heard, they are much more likely to jump onboard even if their idea isn't the one that is taken forward. But they have to be genuinely heard; it can't be an exercise in lip service.'

'So, how do you do that because people can be pretty passionate about their ideas even if they're not the right ideas at that moment.'

'Well, what I like to do with my team is to have a risk log; it's an extension of the decision log where important decisions are discussed and recorded. To ensure a person or persons feel heard, even if they disagree with the decision, their concerns are captured in the log. Then, at our team meetings, we check in to judge the weighting of the risk as the decision is being actioned over time. We ask if the likelihood or impact of the risk increased or decreased, or is it still something we need to be mindful of. What you might find is that the very same people who raised the risk are the ones who take it off the table a couple of weeks down the track. Having said that, there have been a couple of instances where the risk turned out to be real, so we had to introduce a mitigation around it. It's during those times I was glad we had a process to follow.'

'This is good, but even with this in place, does everyone really buy-in all the time?' asked Nathan.

'I don't know,' said Fionn. 'Because I always introduce a team norm when it comes to commitment. I remind them that sometimes within a team, especially a large one, reaching consensus will be nearly impossible. And if we try to reach consensus on every decision, we'll never make any progress; therefore, we're not after consensus, I tell them, we're after commitment. So after we've had a chance to debate the issue and everyone has had the opportunity to wade into the discussion a decision has to be made, right? If we don't make a decision we're demonstrating poor Democratic Leadership.'

'But surely you can be quite autocratic in your approach and make decisions left, right and centre and people will have to commit even if they don't agree with you.'

'Yes, it's true that a leader could take that approach; however, what do you think the impact of that would be?' asked Fionn.

'Well, people will bitch and moan and then eventually leave, I guess.'

'That's exactly right. That's why people have to be genuinely heard and their opinions need to be genuinely taken into account. If someone finds themselves on the wrong end of the decisions being made then they need to be thinking about whether or not they are aligned with the vision and strategy; they also need to be looking at improving their influencing skills. This is something, we as leaders, can help them with,' said Fionn.

'Yeah, that makes sense.'

The Reason We're In Business

A good friend once described it as throwing the person a life-ring, not an anchor.

The digital clock switched over to 5 a.m. Nathan looked at Fionn who was slouched in his chair with his stockinged feet resting on top of a small table. His hands, which cradled a cup of coffee, rested comfortably on his belly. Nathan rubbed his eyes and yawned loudly which caused Fionn to smile.

'Come on,' he said as he sat upright. 'We can do this!' He jumped to his feet and walked about behind the couch and shook his arms. 'Okay,' he said. 'Where were we? Oh yes, we're working our way up the Lencioni's Five Dysfunctions triangle and we've just covered commitment. So, with a lack of commitment there is avoidance of accountability. Now,' he said as his voice picked up energy. 'Without accountability we get low standards.

Plain and simple. If individuals in your team aren't accountable for their work then you have a problem. It could be that they've come from an environment of low trust and they're afraid to take ownership for mistakes; or there might be some other issue where they don't follow through on their work. Either way, it needs to be addressed because if the rest of the team see this kind of behaviour they will absolutely expect that it is corrected. One of the biggest gripes a team has is that poor performance isn't addressed adequately or quickly enough. Don't think for one second that you are the only person seeing this behaviour or being impacted by it.'

'Whoa!' said Nathan. 'This is clearly something you're very passionate about.'

'I certainly am,' Fionn replied in a no-nonsense way. 'All too often I've seen instances where poor behaviour hasn't been addressed by the leader and their boss has had to step in to resolve it. This is not a good look for the leader and it can often cost them their job. In order for a team to work effectively, everyone needs to be pulling their weight.' Fionn paused for a moment and his tone softened. 'Dealing with this can be tricky because, as a leader of people, this has to be done discreetly. There can be several reasons why the person isn't holding themselves accountable or displaying some other poor behaviour that isn't acceptable for a high-performing team. Your job is to help the person get there through coaching and guidance.'

'What if, after everything, even after you try the Commanding Leadership Style, things still haven't improved?'

'Then we're probably leading into the performance management space. This is always uncomfortable for everyone but really necessary for everybody involved, including the person who is being performance managed.' Fionn glanced at the clock again. 'This is something we won't have time to cover, so if you find yourself having to take someone through this process, I would always recommend chatting with Human Resources to get advice about how to successfully execute this process. And remember, the goal is to get the person back on track. A good friend once described it as throwing the person a life-ring, not an anchor.'

Nathan nodded as he thought about his own situation. He was clearly not performing in his role, and he mused, all he really needed was a bit of support, guidance and coaching.

'Always be empathetic through the process,' Fionn said. 'Always be kind and always be clear. Too much kindness is termed ruinous empathy; you know, so much kindness that you get caught up in the person's story and can't help them. It's a fine balance between delivering the message clearly and doing it gently.'

The sound of a car driving too fast pierced the silence between the two friends. Both were tired and struggling to concentrate. Fionn stood up again in an effort to shake off the weight of sleep.

'Of course, then, with accountability, we get full visibility or progress. We have full visibility of mistakes, so we as a team, can resolve them. No blame, just lessons.'

'Ahhh …' said Nathan. 'Just like in your debrief after the rescue.'

'Exactly right. It's really important, to take all these theories that I'm sharing with you and think about how you can use them in practice, so you start getting the results you and your team want. Accountability is good in practice, but how do you do it? Commitment sounds good in practice, but how can you build it?' Fionn glanced yet again at the clock. 'The last of the Five Dysfunctions is inattention to results.'

'Inattention to results?' Nathan repeated.

'That's right. What else are we in business for? The purpose of creating a safe environment, a place where people enjoy coming to work and investing a huge part of their lives, is to deliver results. We have to deliver results or we'll be out of business, right? Of course, those results don't have to be financially based, but we need to be producing something of value. It's all very well creating an environment that panders to everyone's needs, but if we're not delivering, it's just not going to last. It can't!' said Fionn.

'You mean we've spent all this time talking about how leadership is about being kind and creating an environment where people thrive when ultimately it comes down to delivery.'

'Yes, that's exactly what I'm saying.'

'So why can't we just crack the whip a little harder to ensure they do deliver?'

Fionn smiled. 'Well, you tell me.'

Nathan thought about his own experience of working under commanding type leaders and he reminded himself that although the work got done, people were unhappy, the performance was poor and turnover was high. Besides, it wasn't long before he — the good lieutenant, as he liked to think of himself — also wanted to leave.

'Yeah, I get it. We can't make people perform, they have to want to.'

'That's right,' said Fionn. 'In reality, we don't have any control over people, we only have influence and there can be no influence without trust and safety.'

'Got it,' said Nathan.

'So, ultimately, the fifth team dysfunction is inattention to results which leads to status and ego driven, individualised results; *but* with it we get collective and individual results. People are collectively responsible for delivering team goals. We hold each other accountable through feedback and open and honest communication.'

'Great! Thanks for sharing all this. I'm glad you mentioned feedback. This is something I find pretty tricky, the team never listens and it just seems as if they are dismissing everything I say.'

'Crikey! We're cutting it close. It's 5.55 a.m.; don't you need to get to the airport?' Fionn laughed.

'Oh crap!' Nathan jumped up and accidentally knocked his coffee cup with his elbow. 'Oh crap!' he said again.

'Don't worry about it,' said Fionn. 'I'll get a tea towel, you pack your gear.'

The Three Outcomes

She barely looked up.

There were a few cars on the road as they headed for the on-ramp towards the airport. The rain speckled the windscreen and the wipers swished intermittently. Fionn was driving and Nathan sat with his notebook and pen in his lap.

'Thanks for doing this,' said Nathan.

'No problem at all. What else would I be doing?'

'Sleeping!' said Nathan with a laugh.

Fionn chuckled. 'I'm not going to see you for another few years. I want to make the most of our time.'

'Do you think we'll have the time to cover feedback?'

'Sure thing,' said Fionn. I'll have to talk fast though.' He laughed again.

'Okay, the challenge you've got with the team at the moment is a lack of trust. Think of it this way, your relationship is causing so much noise that they can't hear you.'

'What do you mean by noise?'

'Here give me your pad.' Fionn slowed to stop at a set of red lights and grabbed the pen and notebook. He quickly scribbled a simple model on a blank page.

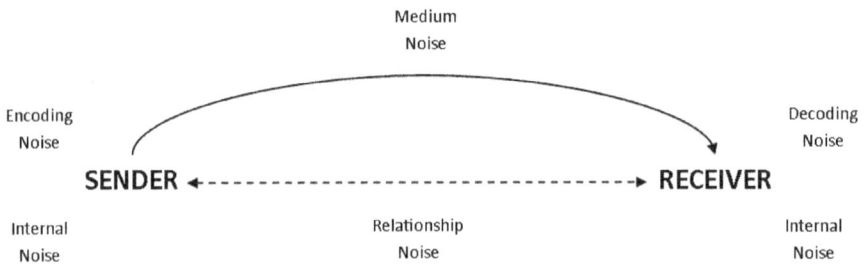

'Person A is the sender and Person B is the receiver,' said Fionn.

Nathan added these extra bits of information to the model.

'At every stage of the communication process there is noise. For example, noise might exist in Person A in the form of bias or lack of cultural awareness or even a lack of understanding about what they are saying. Noise can also exist during the encoding process; that is when the person is formulating what they want to say, the words they choose, etc. to deliver the message. They might, for example, use slang words or acronyms that may lead to confusion.' Fionn looked over at Nathan. 'You with me so far?'

'Yep.' Nathan nodded.

'Okay, noise can also occur in the medium the person chooses to deliver the message.' Fionn reached over and pointed at the arcing line between Person A and B. 'An example of noise within the medium might be autocorrect, if the medium of delivery is text, or the screen freezing on a virtual call, or even if Person A has a speech impediment or a really strong accent. Basically, anything that's going to get in the way of delivering the message.'

Nathan nodded as he scribbled notes. He would have to re-do these he thought to himself; they were barely legible as a result of the motion of the car.

'Then on the flip side, Person B has to decode the message so they need to have the same understanding of the words and phrases used by Person A. They might also have internal biases which will interfere with the integrity of the message delivered by Person A.

But lastly, and this is the important piece to answer the question to your problem, is that noise can also exist because of the relationship between the two parties. If the relationship is fractured, even though the message is delivered with the best intentions, it is going to be received with scepticism.'

'Okay, so what you're saying is that I need to build the relationships before I can even be heard.'

'That's right. You've got an uphill climb ahead of you, but believe me, the effort will be worth it.'

'Cool. I guess I don't have any choice. And to be honest, everything you've shared with me today has given me a renewed sense of motivation. I guess what I was missing was, *how the hell do I do leadership*, and you've really helped me fill in the gaps. Thank you. I really appreciate it.'

'You're welcome. It really is my pleasure. All I'm doing is sharing the lessons my coach has shared with me over the years. Try them, see what works and doesn't work so well, tweak it and go again. It does get easier. But let's quickly talk about feedback.

'Firstly, a feedback conversation should just be conversational in nature. Just like with a coaching conversation, if a person feels like the conversation is staged or a technique is being used on them, the barriers might go up and we may not get the outcome we're after. Speaking of outcomes. There are always three outcomes we have in the back of our minds when stepping into a feedback conversation. The first is about the change in behaviour or the correction of a mistake that we'd like to see. The second is that we are clear in the delivery of our message; clarity is kind, remember? The third is to maintain or even enhance the relationship we have with the person we're giving feedback to.'

'Is that possible, though? To enhance the relationship. People don't tend to like to receive feedback, you know,' said Nathan, unsure that the third outcome was possible.

'That's because people have never learnt to give feedback properly. Most of the time we learn it from how we were given feedback and even though it made us feel crap for a while, we do the exact same thing to others. There's a better way, a much better way.

'I'm going to share a range of different ways of giving feedback. The reason I want to give you the different ways is because human beings are very good at pattern recognition, so if I've only got one way of giving feedback, and I use it a few times, the person is very quickly going to recognise what I'm doing, and may not want to engage fully, which will impact the purpose of our conversation.'

'What's that?' asked Nathan.

'To invite the other person into the conversation, so we can solve the issue together.'

Fionn turned left at the large roundabout and headed past the signs for long-term car parking. He slowed until he saw the signs for rental car return.

'Let's drop off the car and we can pick up the conversation inside.'

'Sounds good,' said Nathan.

Fionn pulled into the rental car return area, found a spot and they jumped out. Nathan dragged his suitcase along the asphalt and Fionn carried his carry-on backpack over his shoulder.

'Good morning,' Fionn said to the person behind the desk. The young woman barely looked up.

'Just returning a car. Here are the keys.'

'Any damage,' she asked with a clear sense of boredom evident in her tone.

'No, no damage,' said Nathan.

'Kay. Thanks,' was all she said. Nathan was left a little put out with her lack of customer service and was about to let her know all about it when Fionn jumped in.

'Thanks a million for making it so easy,' he said gleefully. The woman looked up in confusion, so Fionn continued.

'It must feel pretty good to help remove any unnecessary stress that people might be feeling. I mean travelling is stressful enough as it is, isn't it?'

The woman, still a little perplexed and clearly not used to this kind of conversation, half-smiled. 'S'pose so.'

'Thanks again,' Fionn said as he placed his hand on the counter. 'Have a good one.' With that, he turned away with a smile and walked to the door. Nathan followed, dragging his suitcase behind him.

'You too,' said the woman, loud enough for Fionn to hear as they walked out the door.

They walked to the shuttle bus waiting area. Nathan looked at Fionn a couple of times out of the corner of his eye. He wasn't sure if he should say anything and was still trying to make sense of what he'd just seen. How could he completely ignore such ignorant behaviour? Eventually, he just blurted it out.

'How did you do that? Speaking of feedback, I was ready to give her some and I had no intention of inviting her into the conversation either. And you complimented her?' Nathan was gobsmacked.

Fionn laughed. 'Do you think bawling her out would change anything?' he asked.

'Well, no. But at least I would've felt better,'

'Would you have though?'

Nathan thought about this for a moment or two. 'No, I guess I wouldn't have. I would've exploded and probably stewed over it for the rest of the morning.'

'That's right. Besides, didn't you see the letters written on her forehead?'

Nathan cast his mind back. 'No, I don't recall. Did she have a tattoo or something?'

'No, the letters aren't always visible to everyone, but they were clear to me.'

Nathan was completely perplexed. *Is this what happens when people get severely sleep deprived?*

'What do you mean? What were the letters?' he asked.

'They are the same letters I see on everyone's forehead. M-M-F-I.'

'M-M-F-I,' repeated Nathan.

'That's right,' said Fionn. 'Make Me Feel Important. That's all people want. So even if it's just a brief exchange with someone you may never see again, it costs nothing and it could make their day.'

'Yeah,' said Nathan. 'I like that.'

Just then the shuttle pulled up. They were the only two passengers waiting, so the bus pulled off and they were at the terminal in no time.

The Art of Giving Feedback

Own your own state.

'Thank you for making that so easy,' he said. The woman at the check-in counter beamed a smile back at him.

'You're very welcome, sir. Enjoy your flight,' she said in return.

Nathan felt a rush of good feelings. It was only a brief exchange and he was surprised how, just by simply appreciating another person, how good he could make them feel and how good he felt himself. *M-M-F-I,* he said to himself as he set off in search of Fionn. His flight plan was Dublin to Heathrow, Heathrow to Singapore, Singapore to Sydney, and finally, Sydney to Wellington. It was going to be a long trip, but luckily the stop-over times between flights weren't too bad. He'd definitely be able to catch up on sleep during the Heathrow to Singapore portion of the trip.

He spied Fionn waving at him as he sat at a table in a small airport cafe. 'I got you some tea. When are you boarding?' he asked.

'I've got plenty of time, but I'll head off in forty-five minutes just in case there are any delays getting through security.'

'Sounds good,' said Fionn. 'I've really enjoyed catching up. It's been way too long between drinks,' he joked.

'It certainly has. Way too long. And thanks again for all the advice and guidance. It really has made a big difference. I was dreading going back to work, but now I'm kinda looking forward to it.'

'You'll do well,' said Fionn.

'I know we've only got a few minutes together and I hate to ask you this, but do you think we could finish off the topic of feedback? I just know I'm not going to be able to get this from anywhere else.'

Fionn laughed. 'Of course. Let's do that.'

Fionn looked around and gathered his thoughts. People were coming and going; some were dragging suitcases, others gathered in small isolated clusters as they looked in different directions and tried to figure out where they needed to go next, while others hugged tearful goodbyes.

'Okay, so we talked about how we need to keep feedback as conversational as possible, right?'

Nathan nodded.

'So, in order to do that we need a whole range of different approaches to giving feedback. I'm going to share with you the three essential phases for providing feedback. The first and probably most overlooked phase is Preparation, the second is Formulation, and the third is Exchange. Each of these three phases is essential to an effective feedback conversation.'

'The Preparation Phase is often overlooked so we end up ill-prepared for what we want to say, how we want to say it and how we might overcome any potential pushback or obstacles. There are four steps within the Preparation Phase. These are: **Outcome, Action, Obstacles, and Solution**.

'For Outcome, we complete this sentence: **The outcome I'm after is ...**

'For Action, we complete this sentence: **In order to achieve this outcome I need to ...**

'For Obstacles, we complete this sentence: **The things that might be preventing me from achieving this outcome are ...**

'For Solution, we complete this sentence: **The things I need to put in place to overcome these obstacles are ...**' Fionn paused to let Nathan catch up.

'As you can see, it's pretty straight forward stuff, but thinking this through will really enhance the outcome you're looking to achieve with the other person. Besides, as the boss, a feedback conversation might seem inconsequential to you, but to the person receiving the feedback, it might be the most important conversation they have that day, so we need to spend that five minutes up front to ensure our message lands well.'

Nathan nodded.

'When it comes to the Execution Phase I want to give you a range of different approaches you can take when delivering a message, and the up-front preparation might determine which of these would work best based on the issue that needs to be addressed.

'The first approach is the well-known and often overused Feedback Sandwich. This is a perfectly good way of giving feedback, the problem with it is that if it is overused the person very quickly recognises that every time you pay someone a compliment they tend not to hear it because they're waiting for what you really want to say. So I'd say use it, but use it in balance with the other approaches of giving feedback. The official name for this type of feedback is Commend, Recommend, Commend, by the way.'

'Okay, got it. I'm aware of this one. They use it a lot in Toastmasters,' added Nathan.

'Yes, that's right; it's their preferred method of providing feedback. A second approach to feedback is what I call the You Choose approach. Basically, you say something along the lines of, 'So, Nathan, I've got some good stuff that I know you're going to want to hear and I've also got some other stuff that might be useful for you in the future. Which would you like to hear first?''

'Ohhh! I like that one,' said Nathan as he jotted down the words. 'I like how you phrased it; both options are framed in a positive way.'

'Yeah, that's right. There's nothing negative about feedback, if you think about it.'

Nathan did but couldn't figure out what Fionn meant.

After noticing the perplexed expression on Nathan's face, Fionn continued. 'The only thing that makes feedback positive or negative is the meaning we attribute to it. All feedback is useful because we all have our blind spots, and understanding what another person is seeing, which we might be missing, is useful, is it not?'

Nathan found himself nodding in agreement. 'Then why is it so hard to take sometimes?' he asked.

'What makes feedback hard to take is either the delivery, the relationship, or your own ego.' Fionn laughed.

'Yeah, it's mostly the last one for me, I think.'

'That's okay, something to work on.' Fionn smiled and Nathan nodded in agreement.

'The next approach to feedback I'd like to share with you is the Outcome Approach. Take a moment to compare the steps in these two approaches. The first approach goes like this:

Step 1: We describe the **Problem**.

Step 2: We provide the **Solution**.

Step 3: We share the desired **Outcome**.

Step 4: We check for **Understanding**.

Here's the second approach:

Step 1: We share the desired **Outcome**.

Step 2: We suggest a **Solution**.

Step 3: We check for **Understanding**.

'What's different between these two approaches?' asked Fionn.

'Well, the problem isn't mentioned in the second one and you also changed the wording from *provide the solution* to *suggest a solution*. It's much softer.

'Great stuff! Okay, onto the next one which is the Ask First Approach. With this one we ask the person, 'So, what are your thoughts on how that meeting went?' or 'How did you think you got on with that document?' This way, if the person highlights the area you were thinking about, you can commend them on their insight and then simply ask, and this question is gold, especially when the feedback is task related, 'If you had more time, what would you do differently?''

'So, what if the person doesn't think they could improve on anything or mentions something that is different to what you'd like them to think about?' asked Nathan.

'If that happens, and it will from time to time, then fall back on one of the earlier methods we talked about. The Feedback Sandwich would work pretty well here as a backup. Ready for the next one?' asked Fionn.

'Yep,' Nathan said, flipping a page in his notebook. 'Fire away.'

'The next one is the Next Time approach. This is especially useful when the task is repetitive in nature. For example, a monthly report or a recurring process, something like that. How it works is if the person does a reasonably good job at something, but it's not quite one hundred per cent, and you have to complete it to a certain standard, you praise them on the good work that they've done and you keep the other stuff in your back pocket. Then, when it comes time for the person to repeat the process, you praise them again on the good stuff and draw their attention to the area you'd like them to improve. For example, you might say something along the lines of, 'It's coming up to that time for the report again. You did an amazing job on the layout and capturing the essence of the message we needed to communicate. This time, to build on that, could I ask you to pay particular attention to risks so they can be clearly understood by the board?' or whatever you might say.

'Now, because they're just about to do the report and because you've heaped on the praise, they're much more likely to make the improvements in the areas you suggested. And when they do, you can praise them for that too.'

Nathan laughed. 'You make this stuff sound so easy.'

'Actually, with a bit of practice … and preparation, it is.'

Fionn glanced at his watch. 'Okay, there's two more I want to share with you, but I've only got time for one more before you have to go.' Fionn noticed the look of disappointment on Nathan's face. 'But don't worry, the last one will magically appear for you.'

Nathan's smile was fleeting. He knew his old friend was up to something. He wished he had more time.

'The next one is the S.B.I. approach. It stands for Situation, Behaviour, Impact. It's a useful model to help you structure what you'd like to say. So, for example, it might sound something like, 'Nathan, in the meeting yesterday — *situation* — I noticed you dominated a lot of the conversation — *behaviour* — and this caused everyone else to not speak up and share their views — *impact*.' Can you see how that works?'

Nathan nodded. 'Yes, I like it.'

'You can also use it to give praise. You might say, 'Nathan, in the meeting yesterday — *situation* — I noticed you asked some really great questions — *behaviour* — and this caused everyone else to go deeper with their thoughts — *impact*.

'Okay,' said Fionn, rubbing his hands together. 'Here's the very last piece of the puzzle before you have to go to your gate; the Exchange Phase. When it comes to the exchange phase, if you follow this process you can't go wrong:

1. **Own your own state**. Make sure you're in the right frame of mind to hold a feedback conversation. Make sure you're not bringing any baggage that doesn't need to be there into the space.

2. **Deliver your feedback**. Choose your method of delivery and share it.

3. **Ask**. Ask them what their thoughts are. Sometimes a person doesn't need to be asked and that's great. Other times they might stay silent. Remember the ultimate goal of a feedback conversation is to invite the other person into the conversation, so if they're quiet you have to ask them for their thoughts.

4. **Understand and empathise**. During this stage of the conversation they might be upset or they might disagree. That's okay. Your job here is to simply paraphrase what they say so they feel heard and understood.

5. **Way forward**. Once the person has shared their thoughts and you've had a chance to discuss this openly you move onto the solution. What things will the person do differently? for example.

6. **Inspire**. This is the last step. Sometimes the person might feel a little downtrodden depending on how they received the feedback. It's your job to remind them of the contribution they make to the team and that they are a valuable member.

'Follow that formula and you can't go wrong. Take your time with it though, especially the fourth step, don't feel the need to rush to a solution. It'll come.' Fionn was silent while Nathan finished his notes. When he stopped writing he looked up. Fionn nodded a single nod and Nathan responded in kind. He clicked the top of his pen, closed his notebook and put it back in his carry-on backpack.

The Millennials

Slán leat, mo chara.

The two friends walked quickly in the direction of the gate when Fionn remembered something Nathan had asked during the rescue.

'You asked about how to give feedback to millennials.'

'Oh yeah, any quick words of wisdom?'

'Here are a couple of quick pointers for you. Millennials tend to value feedback a little differently than us oldies.

- **Focus on development:** Frame the feedback as a way to help them grow professionally. In most instances, millennials are ambitious and want to learn, so show them how the feedback furthers their career goals.

- **Be specific and actionable:** Don't just say something is wrong, explain how it can be improved. Give clear examples and suggestions for them to move forward, they'll appreciate that much more.

- **Use positive reinforcement:** Start with acknowledging their strengths and positive aspects of the work. This sets a positive tone and shows you value their contributions. Think of using the Feedback Sandwich, for example.

- **Use a collaborative approach:** Instead of dictating solutions, ask for their ideas on how to improve. This fosters a sense of ownership and makes them more receptive to the feedback. This is pretty much the approach we've been talking about anyway.

- **Be timely and specific:** Address issues sooner rather than later, while the situation is still fresh. Be specific about what needs improvement.

- **Lastly, use respectful communication:** Avoid accusatory language or a condescending tone. Focus on the work itself and use 'I' statements to communicate your observations.

'I hope that's not too much for you to remember,' Fionn said and chuckled.

'Nope, I think I've got it. Focus on development, be specific and actionable, use positive reinforcement, use a collaborative approach, be timely and specific, and use respectful communication,' Nathan recited.

'Just one more thing,' said Nathan. They'd reached the security gates and Nathan was reaching into his black combats to retrieve his ticket and passport. 'You mentioned using *I* statements when using respectful communication. What's an *I* statement?'

'Trust in the magic. I promise it will appear.'

The two friends hugged and Nathan felt a wrenching in his chest. He'd miss his friend dearly, and try as he might, he couldn't find the words to fully express his appreciation for everything his friend had shared with him.

'Slán leat, mo chara,' said Fionn, using the traditional Irish form of goodbye. It's literal translation is *safe with you*.

'Slán abhaile,' said Nathan in reply. *Safe home*.

The Dream

You don't matter.

Nathan made his way through the alcohol, sunglasses, and gadget shops. He glanced around purposefully. There was one item he needed before he boarded his flight. Then he spied it. He made his way to the bookstore and found the stationery section in the back. He picked up a Moleskine A4 notebook. Ivory pages, 80 gsm, elastic closure ribbon marker, expandable back pocket.

Perfect! he said to himself. He paid for it at the counter and just as he was about to turn away he saw it. He saw the letters MMFI on the young server's forehead.

'You're doing a really good job, you know that? Thank you,' said Nathan.

The young man looked up at him in astonishment and a smile crept across his face. Nathan had already turned to walk away when he heard the server call after him. 'Thank you, have a safe flight.'

It was Nathan's turn to smile and he took a moment to enjoy those good feelings as he casually made his way to his gate. He had plenty of time and even though he was exhausted he also felt strangely energised. The waiting area for his flight was starting to fill up, so he found a water station and filled his water bottle. After finding a seat with a good view of the counter, he settled down to wait for the boarding call.

After a few minutes his eyes started to feel heavy and he felt his head drop. He woke with a fright and looked around in embarrassment. A little girl sitting opposite him with her parents giggled and covered her mouth. Nathan stuck his tongue out at her and she giggled some more under her hand. Not ready to fall asleep, Nathan was reaching into the front pocket of his carry-on backpack to review his notes when he felt a book.

That question, *Did you pack your own luggage?* shot through his mind. He pulled out the book and read the cover. **FIRST, LEAD YOURSELF: PRACTICAL TOOLS TO UNLEASH YOUR LEADERSHIP POTENTIAL**. Nathan couldn't help but smile. He noticed a Post-it note sticking out from the side of the book. He flicked to the page. *See ... magic happens all the time* were the words handwritten on the Post-it note. Nathan tore off the note and read the subtitle on the page: **The 'I' Statement**. He couldn't help but laugh yet again.

He read through the chapter and flicked through the rest of the book nodding his agreement as he skimmed through the contents. It wasn't long before his flight was called for boarding. Nathan packed the book into his bag. He made his way towards the boarding gate glancing quickly over his shoulder at the seating area, and satisfied he hadn't left anything behind, boarded the plane.

The flight from Dublin to Heathrow was uneventful. Nathan allowed himself to close his eyes for the few minutes it took to cross the Irish Sea, but before he knew it they were making their descent.

He only had a couple of hours between flights, and once he was satisfied he knew where his next boarding gate was, he wandered around looking at the over-priced shops. Before heading to the gate he bought himself a packet of toffees as a little treat for the long flight to Singapore.

The flight was full and it took a while before his boarding category was called, but he didn't mind. He waited patiently and observed those around him. The waiting patiently thing surprised him; normally he would be agitated and vying for the best position to be in so he could be first. This amused him as he noticed a handful of others doing the same. He smiled to himself and wondered if he looked as idiotic as they did right now.

Before putting his bag in the overhead locker he unpacked his toffees, a pen and his new Moleskine notebook. He rested it on his lap, turned his phone on to flight mode, and once the plane was in the air, he put in his noise cancelling earbuds, and closed his eyes for a well-deserved sleep.

'I'm going out for a drive,' he said as he popped his head in the sitting room door. His parents, siblings and grandparents were sitting around the room watching television with paper-thin crowns on their heads and glasses of beer in their hands. He felt obliged to join them, but he really didn't want the company.

'Okay, honey,' said his mother and he closed the door.

'Is he okay?' he overheard his grandmother asking. He didn't wait for any response. He wasn't okay, but he didn't know why. His mind felt it was being pulled apart in every direction.

Nathan found himself driving his 1989 Honda Jazz through the Wicklow Mountains and leaving the world behind him. He meandered along narrow roads lined with stone walls and continued so that even these reminders of life were far behind him. Eventually, he pulled off the road and reversed into a lay-by. He was at the peak of Sally Gap surrounded by darkness and quiet. The only sound was the wind blowing in the trees and he just sat there staring into the darkness replaying the events of the last few days in his head.

Everything seemed to happen all at once and within a week he had been fired from his job and had broken up with his girlfriend. Once again it was his anger and frustration that took over and led him to making stupid decisions. He banged the steering wheel with his fists.

'What is wrong with people?' he screamed. 'Why do they have to be such arseholes?' His outburst was over as quickly as it had begun. There was a part of him that knew it wasn't other people who were the problem, but that was drowned out by anger. He sat there quietly for how long he didn't know. He counted three cars going past during that time. Eventually, he sighed heavily, turned the key in the ignition and drove onto the road.

He travelled in silence back the way he had come, acutely aware of the giant fir trees bordering the road.

'You don't matter.' Nathan jumped awake with a start. He looked around him wide-eyed. People were sitting quietly in their seats plugged into a movie or reading a book. The constant hum of the plane was the only sound he could hear through his earbuds. He flicked through the in-flight movies trying to distract himself, but his mind kept going back to those words, *You don't matter.*

What surprised him most of all was the tension he held in his body during the dream dissipated upon hearing the words. He couldn't figure out where they came from and couldn't place the voice; it seemed as if it came from outside himself but from within at the same time.

He shook his head, grabbed his phone and opened the notes app, scrolled to the top of the page and placed it on the seat tray. Then he opened his Moleskine notebook and started to transcribe his scattered notes into a more legible and coherent form.

Before he knew it, the plane was making its descent into Singapore Airport. He realised he had slept through the meals, and upon looking down at his notes, saw that he didn't get very far.

Once the plane had landed, Nathan stood up, stretched and recovered his bag from the overhead locker. He noticed an older Chinese woman struggling with her bags, so he reached over and retrieved them for her. She nodded her thanks and Nathan smiled in return. He was getting used to paying attention to those good feelings he got from helping others. *You don't matter.* Those words again. The message behind them was becoming clear. *Maybe, it's not that you don't matter but that other people matter more.* Nathan's mind poured over this thought. Part of it felt right but part of it didn't. *Other people matter more,* he repeated to himself. Surely that wasn't right.

After proceeding through his airport routine of finding out where his next boarding gate was, and double-checking the gate on the departures screen, he suddenly became aware of his hunger. As soon as he'd found a small cafe, he ordered tofu noodles and a green tea. He smiled at the man behind the counter who took his order before he found a table to sit at.

Among the throng of people going by he noticed a couple of young parents dragging their two small boys along with them while they wrestled with their suitcases. One of the boys had a football that he kept dropping. His mother repeatedly admonished him about holding onto the ball. He dropped it again and she lost her temper. She dropped to his height, grabbed his arm and turned him to face her. The boy's eyes kept following the ball and his mother kept pulling him back to look at her. Tears streamed down his face and all he could say was, 'My ball. My ball is gone.'

Just then, an older man emerged from the crowd and held out the ball. 'Does this belong to anybody?' The little boy reached out for the ball, but the man was quick, he backed away, just out of the boy's reach, but still presenting the ball to the child. After a moment of hesitation the boy reached for the ball again. The man dropped the ball onto his foot where he expertly held it as he balanced on one foot. Nathan couldn't help smiling at this spectacle. The young boy reached for the ball a third time, but once again he wasn't quick enough. This time the older man bounced the ball from one foot to the other and the child watched in amazement. Eventually, the man held the ball under his foot, and seeing his chance, the boy lunged for it. The older man rolled the ball away and danced the ball from one foot to the other. The little boy's sibling joined in and together they tried to retrieve the ball, but the man magically kept it from their grasp. Eventually, the two boys lay on their backs laughing hysterically. At this point the old man picked up the ball and handed it to the first child.

'What do you say to the nice man?' asked the mother.

'Thank you, mister,' they said in thick Australian accents.

'You're welcome,' replied the man before he turned to where his wife was waiting and she playfully slapped him on the arm as they disappeared into the crowd. The young parents took the boys by their hands and continued their journey, all signs of despair were forgotten.

You don't matter. Nathan heard the words again. This time he smiled; he got it. It's not that you don't matter, it's that when you look out for others and show them that *they* matter, then you will matter more to them. Stop trying to make yourself matter, just focus on making others matter. The same uncomfortable feeling he felt when Stephen gripped his hand before he was taken away in the ambulance returned for an instant before being replaced by a lightness in his chest. This feeling of discomfort was the shift from putting himself first, to putting others first. Feeling the lightness in his chest affirmed he was on the right track. To Nathan it simply felt like a more natural way of being.

The Man From Cork

Understanding yourself is probably the most important of them all.

Nathan broke the eight-hour flight from Singapore to Sydney by watching a movie, transcribing his notes, and drawing diagrams to make the information more digestible, as well as getting some sleep.

He opened his eyes and looked around. His notebook was still open on the table. At the top of the page were the words My Leadership Philosophy. This is where it all got too hard. He closed his notes and checked the remaining flight time; fifty-five minutes to go. He yawned and stretched as best as he could in the seat.

'Excuse me.' It was the man sitting next to him. 'Do you mind if I disturb you? I just need to pop to the loo.'

'Of course,' said Nathan. He jumped out of his seat and let the man out. Once he was back in his seat, he flicked through documentaries and short TV shows to see if there was anything of interest to pass the time until they landed. Nothing jumped out at him.

'Thank you,' said his seating companion.

'No problem at all.' Nathan jumped up and the man sat down in his seat.

'Is that an Irish accent I hear?' asked the man.

'It is, yeah. Where are you from yourself?'

'I'm from Cork,' the man replied. 'I'm David, by the way. And where are you from? Is that a Wicklow accent, I'm hearing?'

Nathan laughed. 'It is, indeed. You've got a great ear. I'm Nathan.'

'I've just travelled around the place, is all,' said David. 'Tell me, I noticed a few of your notes. Are you into leadership?'

'Trying to be,' Nathan replied sheepishly. 'I'm just returning home from a trip to Ireland and I had an amazing experience that really opened my eyes to what leadership is actually about. Is it something you're interested in yourself?'

'You could say that,' said David light-heartedly. 'I've actually got a doctorate in it.'

'You're kiddin' me,' said Nathan as he sat up in his chair. 'Tell me about it. What was it based on?'

'Are you sure I won't bore you?' asked David.

'No, no. Please. I'm really interested.'

'Well, in simple terms I have tried to determine what makes the best leaders the best. So I spent two weeks each with ten leaders. I followed them around at work. I sat quietly in every meeting they had. I lived with their families and slept in their homes. I was like a limpet; everywhere they went, I went for the whole two weeks.'

'Wow! That's amazing. It must've been a helluva experience. And how cool that they let you do it, too.'

'Oh yes, I was very lucky. Not only were they great great leaders, but they were great people too. Very generous with their time and they did their very best to help other people when they could.'

Nathan nodded his agreement. *You don't matter,* he said the words to himself. 'So what did you learn from them?'

'Too many things to cover in ...' David looked at the miniature plane on his screen. 'Thirty-five minutes.' He laughed.

'I can imagine,' said Nathan. 'Who was the most successful of all the leaders you studied and what made them so good?'

'I was measuring their success as leaders by calculating the company's revenue in proportion to their staff size and there was one CEO who stood out more than the rest,' replied David. 'He was such a kind and thoughtful man, but he did the least work of any of them.' David laughed uproariously and slapped his knee.

Nathan laughed along with him. David's personality was infectious and even though they were only talking for a brief period of time, Nathan found he liked him immensely.

'You're kidding, right?' asked Nathan. 'Surely he had to do something.'

'I'm joking a wee bit,' he replied. 'But not by much. The one thing that stood out more than anything else was when people came into his office to ask his advice, but he never gave it to them. He would ask questions and guide them towards an answer and then he'd say, every single time, 'Make sure you use your best judgement now, won't you?' And that was it. He was a master at it and his people loved him.'

'It sounds like he used the coaching style of leadership a lot,' said Nathan.

David looked impressed. 'Yes, that's exactly what he did. Of course, he ensured his people had everything they needed and the environment was correctly set up so that everyone knew what they were doing. He encouraged people to come to him with ideas when they got stuck and also when they had no ideas. Everyone trusted him and felt comfortable in his presence.'

'Wow, that sounds like leadership in action, right there.' Nathan's eyes glazed as he imagined himself being that kind of leader.

'So, what else are you working on there?' David asked as he pulled Nathan out of his reverie.

'Oh, actually I'm just working on my leadership philosophy. But I'm a little stuck.'

At that moment the air hostess walked by and told everyone and no one in particular to fasten their seatbelts for landing, and put up their tray tables and seat backs. She glanced in their row as Nathan was putting away his tray table and giving his seatbelt a little tug.

'Tell me a little more about what you know about the Leadership Styles,' David said. That's a good place to start.'

Nathan gave David a quick overview of how, based on Fionn's guidance, he had structured the styles.

'It sounds like you've got everything you need there,' David replied.

The mechanical sound of the wheels indicated they were close to landing.

'In the interest of time, can I make a suggestion?' David asked.

'Of course.'

'What's worked for others is taking a moment to explore who you currently are as a leader, warts and all. This is what we refer to as your Actual Self. Then explore who you'd like to be as a leader, don't worry if you're not there yet, or even if you're unsure about how to get there, write it down. This is what we refer to as your Ideal Self. Once you establish these *two selves.*' David used air quotes around these two words. 'You see where they overlap. These are your strengths. Then, explore where they don't overlap, these are your gaps, or your opportunities for improvement.'

Nathan was frantically capturing everything David was saying. The pen drifted up the length of the page as the plane bounced gently before settling down on the runway.

'Okay, great. What do I do once I've done this?'

'The next couple of steps are easy. Once you have all this information you can go ahead and create what's called your Learning Agenda. It's your strategy or plan to help you build on your strengths, those things you're already doing well, and to close the gaps, your work-ons to become your ideal leader.'

'This is great,' Nathan said as he continued to write hastily. 'But how do I develop my Leadership Philosophy?'

The plane came to a standstill and the seatbelt sign turned off with a familiar ping.

'Once you've captured all this information, re-look at the description of the leadership styles, paying particular attention to those attributes you mentioned, and jot down the key words which come to you and capture what a good leader looks like. Using these words as a guide, craft your Leadership Philosophy.'

'Okay,' said Nathan, a little sceptical. 'It's that easy, huh?'

David laughed. 'It's only easy once you've done the work to exploring *your selves.*' He made air quotes with his fingers again. 'And explored your strengths, etc. It's like most things, once you've mastered the fundamentals, the rest doesn't seem so hard.'

Nathan was nodding and already thinking about what makes a great leader.

'If I was to sum up leadership it would be this: Understand yourself, understand others, do the basics really well. That's about building relationships, providing clarity, linking your plan to a vision, putting guidelines in place to help the team self-manage, delegate well and always provide feedback and praise. The rest of leadership comes down to problem-solving skills, and how to approach these challenges can be learnt from others or through experience.'

Nathan jotted this down as people started to make their way down the aisle.

'One last thing,' David said. 'Understanding yourself is probably the most important of all. Understanding what your triggers are, how you regulate your emotions, building resilience, and having strong communication skills are essential. These need to be habits, so they don't take up too much cognitive energy. It's when we're trying hard just to be present and trying to deal with complexity, and sometimes chaos.' David laughed his warm laugh. 'That's when it can all get too much and the wheels start to fall off.'

Nathan nodded at the familiarity of the words. 'It's funny you should mention that,' he said. 'That's exactly the theme of the book *First, Lead Yourself* that a friend of mine gave me to read.'

'It sounds like good advice,' David said. They were standing up now and retrieving their bags from the overhead lockers. 'That reminds me,' he said. 'Here you go.' David handed Nathan a hardcover book. Nathan mouthed the words, '*The Art of Deliberate Success* by Dr. David Keane.' The cover was adorned with a range of colourful paper cranes.

Nathan paused to look at David. 'Wow! Is this you?'

David laughed again. 'I thought you might enjoy reading it.'

People were starting to get impatient as they stood in the aisle waiting for the two new friends to finish chatting. Nathan led the way with David behind him. For the first time in his life he wished the flight had taken longer.

They picked up their bags and said their goodbyes. David was spending a couple of days in Sydney with family before continuing his journey to New Zealand.

'It has been a real pleasure meeting you,' said Nathan. 'Thank you so much for your advice. I just wish I had the time to run my Leadership Philosophy by you to get your thoughts.'

David smiled. 'It's been a real pleasure meeting you too,' he said. 'The only person your Leadership Philosophy matters to, is you. Give it a go. Review it every morning and allow it to influence how you show up every day. Eventually, it will become part of you and you will become authentic in your words and in your actions. You may find that you modify it a little as you start to put it into practice, but the key is to write it out and remember ...' David paused and smiled. 'Use your best judgement.' He laughed his big hearty laugh again. The two new friends shook hands and parted ways.

The Beginning

I can see clearly now the rain has gone.

The flight from Sydney to Wellington was largely uneventful. As excited as he was about getting back home, Nathan felt like the walking dead. In between naps he reviewed his notes, completed the exercise David suggested to him, and created his Leadership Philosophy.

It was early on Thursday morning when he finally arrived back in Wellington. Completely exhausted, he propped himself up against a pillar next to the baggage carousel and waited for his bag to arrive. After clearing customs with nothing to declare he popped the last of his toffees in his mouth as he walked into the cool morning air.

The shuttle wasn't long in arriving and Nathan, along with the other passengers, loaded their luggage and crammed into the seats for the short ride to the long-term car park.

Once he'd found his car, he slumped in the front seat, dropped his head back against the headrest and sighed heavily. After a moment he opened his eyes and started the car. He paused for a moment, took out his phone and searched for a song. Connected by Bluetooth, the trance-like sound of the piano came through the speakers.

He exited the car park tapping his fingers on the steering wheel in time with the music. The unmistakable voice of Stephen Ó Maonlaí filled the car. He sang about how the clouds have lifted and the sun is now shining through, and he can finally see beyond the obstacles in his way.

Nathan sang along to the gentle melody as he made his way through the airport onto State Highway 1. The sun was rising over the waterfront and it did indeed appear it was going to be a bright sunny day. The backing vocalists joined in and gently and unmistakably lifted the tempo of the tune. Nathan's voice picked up in unison.

The song continued to rise in tempo, and with it Nathan could feel his energy returning. He tapped the steering wheel harder and his foot stomped the floor in rhythm with the tune.

The song was reaching its crescendo and the saxophone took over; Nathan's energy was building with it. He smiled to himself and for the first time in a long time he was looking forward to his future.

The Interview

It starts with building trust.

'Tell us, Nathan, what does being a leader mean to you?'

Nathan sat in the interview room feeling a genuine sense of confidence. Confidence built on experience and not just pomp and arrogance. The role he was being interviewed for was a stretch for him, but it was the right next step for his career and personal growth.

Since he had returned from Ireland, Nathan had worked hard to implement everything he had learnt. He continued to read his Leadership Philosophy every morning and he rehearsed how he would "show up" to the day ahead in his mind. Following the guidance Fionn gave him about how to build a team he eventually started to make inroads, and after being consistent with his behaviour and his message, he slowly started to build that essential ingredient of trust. It wasn't all plain sailing, and he certainly felt they were testing him at times, but as he fell back on his new found skills he was able to navigate these challenges without too much difficulty.

Not everyone in the team was happy that others were now starting to accept Nathan into the team, and their behaviour reflected this. After a few conversations with Claudia, and guidance from his Human Resources partner, he stepped into those difficult conversations, which eventually led to these members of the team moving onto different things. Part of him felt as if he had let them down, but another part recognised this is sometimes an unfortunate part of the job as a leader. What surprised Nathan the most was the change in mood of the team when the old team members moved on. Things seemed more relaxed; there was more laughter among the team and the team as a whole was more productive.

Nathan enjoyed building the relationships with the team more than he thought he would. The conversations were a little stilted at first, but gradually, as Nathan started opening up, they did too. The hard part, he found, was sitting back and allowing others to debate topics he was passionate about. In the past, he would have dominated the conversation and largely got his own way, but he had to admit the ideas and solutions that the team came up with were far superior to his own. Providing that safe space for the team to fill and creating real clarity allowed Nathan to sit back and observe. Every now and then he had to jump in to make slight course corrections, but by and large the team were now leading themselves.

He continued to stay in touch with Fionn and David, who continued to inspire his leadership style. On Fionn's advice, Nathan engaged a coach who he found to be an invaluable source of guidance.

'To me, a leader is someone who delivers in alignment with the organisational strategy. They do this by creating an environment in which the team thrives and knows how the decisions they make today influence the direction of the organisation tomorrow.'

The interview panel nodded while jotting down Nathan's answer.

'So how do you create an environment in which teams thrive?'

'It starts with building trust. But not just predictability trust, vulnerability trust. The type of trust among the team that allows us to put our hands up if we make a mistake or need help without fear of ridicule or punishment. It's the same type of trust that enables the team themselves to hold each other accountable for behaviour or decisions that don't align with the team values.'

The panel continued to record what Nathan was saying and as the interview progressed it felt more like a seminar on leadership than an interview. Nathan didn't get the job he applied for, but he was offered a more senior role within the company which he gladly, albeit nervously, accepted.

Epilogue

The thought was as relentless as the waves lapping against the sea wall.

Tadgh sat on a bench staring out to sea. He pulled his arms closer around him as he tried to stay warm. It shouldn't have been this cold in the summer, but the wind chill made even a sunny day unpleasant. One part of him wanted to find somewhere shielded from the wind and he wondered if that place would also shield him from his thoughts. Another part told him he deserved to be cold, he deserved to suffer. The bench he was sitting on was placed on what was once tidal swamp land, which was caused by the most powerful earthquake ever recorded in New Zealand history. That was back in 1855, and he couldn't imagine the Herculean effort it took to reclaim all this land after such a cataclysmic event. He couldn't bring himself to care. Past history was the furthest thing from his mind; recent history was all that concerned him now. *How could I mess it all up?* The thought was as relentless as the waves lapping against the sea wall.

People passed by in groups of twos and threes laughing and joking during their lunch-time walk. Others ran past breathing heavily pushing themselves that bit harder knowing they were close to finishing their afternoon jog. He imagined what he might look like to a passer-by — sullen? Dejected? He wondered if anyone would sit next to him and ask if he was okay — ask him to tell his story. What would he tell them? Would he tell them that two months ago he secured his dream job? Would he tell them he was running a team of software engineers, testers, business analysts and architects and now he was messing it all up? Or would he tell them to go and …

A man sat on the bench next to him and opened his salad container, carefully protecting it against the wind. Tadgh ignored him. He shifted uneasily on the bench and turned to ward off the growing harshness of the wind. He looked around at the faces passing by hoping for some form of eye contact, hoping that someone would recognise his pain. None did.

'Oh sorry,' said the man. He reached over and retrieved his napkin that had blown into Tadgh's lap.

'No problem,' said Tadgh.

'It looks like you're having a tough day,' said the man.

Tadgh bristled. *Be careful what you ask for.*

Nathan gave a half-hearted laugh.

'You could say that. I'm about two months into my dream job and I'm failing miserably.'

'Oh,' said the man. 'Perhaps I can help.'

He reached over to shake Tadgh's hand.

'I'm Nathan.'

Nathan's Notes
How to Lead Others

Chapter Reference: The Wicklow Mountains

Understanding Leadership

- *We model leadership from others who have led us in the past.*
- *We always go back to what we know under times of stress.*
- *Leadership is a very stressful role, therefore it's important to be able to manage this so energy and focus can be used for better problem-solving and decision-making.*
- *Remember to pause — remember to respond, not to react.*
- *Because leadership skills are developed and stored in the limbic system (emotional part of the brain), we have to develop them in a specific way — it's more a case of relearning on top of old deeply ingrained habits. Therefore, changing leadership skills requires lots of practice and lots of repetition.*
- *Feedback from your peers and your team is vitally important when developing these skills.*
- *Laissez-faire leadership can work, but on its own it is a weak form of leadership. Leadership must be purposeful.*

Chapter Reference: The First Lesson

Dealing with Negative Thoughts[1]

How we deal with negative thoughts can determine our effectiveness when dealing with other people and external challenges.

The 6 Step process for dealing with negative thoughts is:

1. *Write down the thought.*

2. *Ask yourself, 'Is that true?'*

3. *If yes, ask yourself again, 'Can you absolutely know that it's true?'*

4. *Write down the answers to these questions:*

   a. *How do you react when you think it's true? Who do you become?*

   b. *How do you treat others?*

5. *Write down the answer to this question: Who would you be without that thought?*

6. *Lastly, turn it around. Write down the opposite of the thought and check how true the new thought feels. Does it feel as true or truer than the original thought?*

---

[1] Loving What Is by Byron Katie

Chapter Reference: The Art of Delegation

Effective Delegation[2]	

The purpose of the Delegation model is to set people up to succeed.

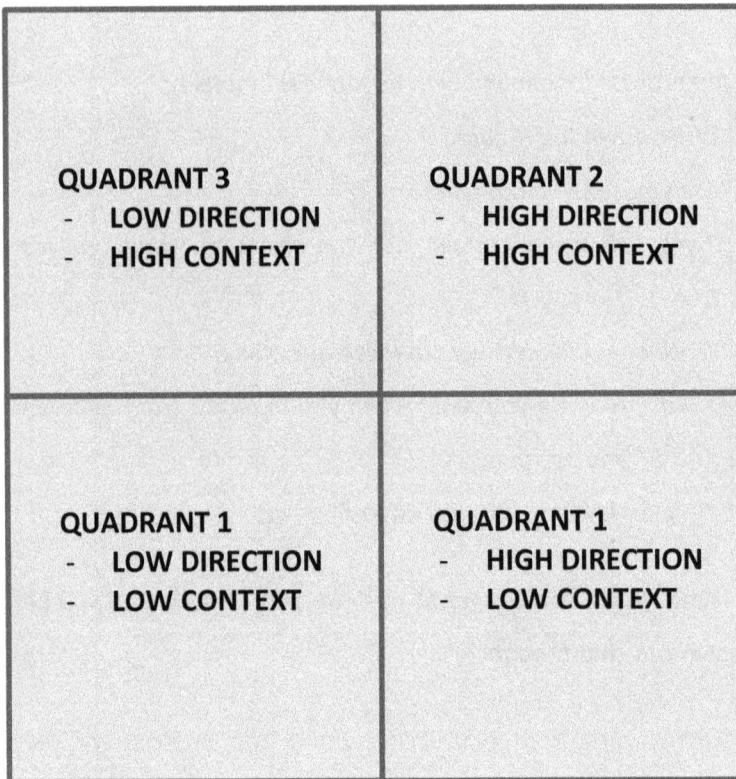

QUADRANT 3	QUADRANT 2
- LOW DIRECTION	- HIGH DIRECTION
- HIGH CONTEXT	- HIGH CONTEXT
QUADRANT 1	**QUADRANT 1**
- LOW DIRECTION	- HIGH DIRECTION
- LOW CONTEXT	- LOW CONTEXT

[2] Situational Leadership by Ken Blanchard

Chapter Reference: The Art of Delegation

Effective Delegation

Q1 Notes

- *Be clear; don't waste time on superlative information. Arrange a check-in with them in no greater than 3 day's time. Always be available for questions.*

Q2 Notes

- *Be clear and add more context, explain the 'why'.*
- *Give them more time before checking-in (depending on the risk profile of the task and their competence).*
- ***The 30% – 80% feedback model is useful here.***

Q3 Notes

- *State the problem and outcome. Ask them for their thoughts. Check for risks and ask necessary questions.*
- *Use the boat analogy to balance risks and learning.*
  - *Above the waterline: Conversation after.*
  - *Below the waterline: Conversation beforehand.*

Q4 Notes

- *Give the problem to the person; they have the capability and right attitude to do a good job.*
- *Maintain a strong connection; continue to build the relationship.*

Chapter Reference: The Art of Delegation

The XDS Model of Delegation[3]

Step 1: *Keep a record of everything you do during your week.*

Step 2: *Divide a blank piece of paper with a line down the middle.*

Step 3: *On the left-hand side, write down only those things that you can do.*

Step 4: *On the right-hand side, write down everything else.*

Step 5: *Use XDS on all the tasks on the right-hand side.*

    a.   X – CUT

    b.   D – DELEGATE

    c.   S – SYSTEMATISE

Note: *Your team might not be ready for the delegated task; however, through coaching and support this task can gradually be transferred to them.*

---

[3] From 6 to 7 Figures by Dan Martell

Chapter Reference: The Art of Delegation

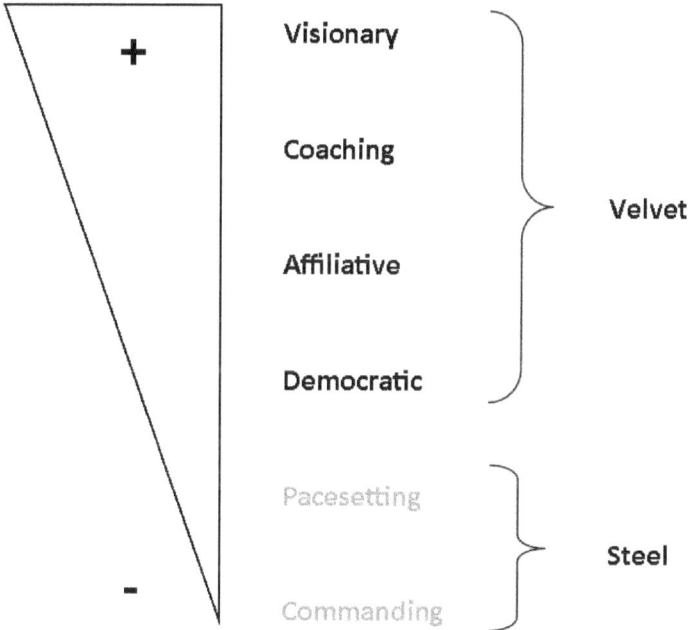

Leadership Styles Overview[4]

There are 6 leadership styles. In order of "most positively impactful", these are:

+

Visionary

Coaching

Affiliative

Democratic

Velvet

Pacesetting

Commanding

Steel

-

[4] The New Leaders by Daniel Goleman

The Visionary Leadership Style[4]

Of all the leadership styles, this style appears to be the most strongly positive.

Environmental Impact: *The visionary leadership style excels at igniting a shared dream or vision within a team. This is especially valuable when an organization lacks direction or needs a fresh course. By articulating a compelling future state, a visionary leader can inspire and energize a team to move towards a common goal.*

When to Use: *When changes require a new vision, or when clear direction is needed.*

Traits: *Empathy, self-confidence, change agent, transparency, honesty/integrity.*

Things to Note About the Style: *This style can backfire when working with highly experienced teams or peers. New Leaders might be seen as lacking expertise or out of touch with the team's established goals. This can breed cynicism, especially if the leader comes across as overly directive. The result can be a demotivated team and ultimately, lead to poor performance.*

[4] The New Leaders by Daniel Goleman

Chapter Reference: The Visionary

The Visionary Leadership Style[5]

Also, making changes or suggesting a new direction too soon without a valid reason can cause people to push back and refuse to commit to the vision.

The current environment should determine where you should focus your energy.

	Action	Consolidation
More Learning	**Realignment***	**Sustaining Success**
More Doing	**Start-up**	**Turnaround**

* Realignment can also be interpreted as a team or organisational restructure.

[5] The First 90 Days by Michael Watkins

The Coaching Leadership Style[4]

This is a highly positive leadership style.

Environmental Impact: This style prioritizes long-term development over short-term gains. By fostering loyalty, a strong company culture, and aligning individual aspirations with organisational goals, which ultimately drive positive bottom-line results.

When to Use: Effective coaching goes beyond addressing short-term issues. It's a strategic investment that builds long-term capabilities in team members. When done well, it fosters not only improved performance, but also increased self-confidence and autonomy.

Traits: Emotional self-awareness, unconditional positive regard, empathy, rapport building, listening and asking questions.

Things to Note About the Style: By exploring a person's dreams, life goals, and career aspirations, we can create a more fulfilling work experience for them, leading to increased engagement and productivity.

---

[4] The New Leaders by Daniel Goleman

Chapter Reference: The Coach

The Coaching Leadership Style

A note of caution: While coaching can be a powerful leadership tool, its misuse can veer into micromanagement or excessive control. This stifles team member confidence and ultimately hinders performance. Perhaps more than any other style, effective coaching requires significant leadership skill.

The GROW Model

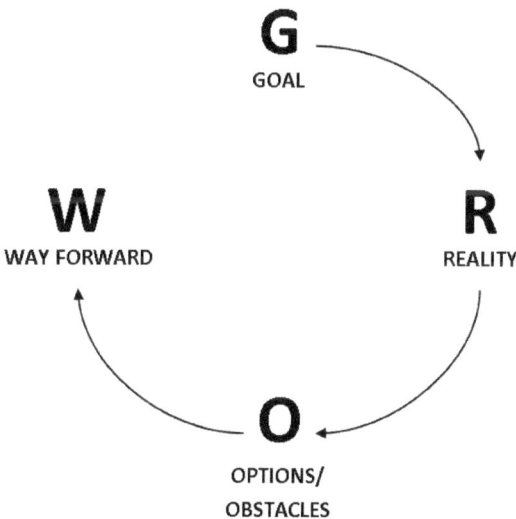

G
GOAL

W
WAY FORWARD

R
REALITY

O
OPTIONS/
OBSTACLES

The Coaching Leadership Style

Coaching Conversation Questions

Goal
- *How would you like things to be?*
- *What would good look like in this situation?*
- *What would be a good outcome here?*

Reality
- *What does the current situation look like?*
- *How is the problem showing up for you?*
- *How is this impacting you right now?*

Options
- *What are some of the solutions you've tried?*
- *What are options you could consider?*
- *What else could you do?*

Obstacles
- *What's preventing you from doing that?*
- *What's getting in the way?*
- *What's preventing you from moving forward?*

Way Forward
- *What small step can you take to move closer to the goal?*
- *How can you start making it the way you want it to be?*
- *What can you do today to achieve your outcome?*

Chapter Reference: The Affiliate

The Affiliative Leadership Style[4]

This leadership style has a positive impact on the environment.

Environmental Impact: This leadership style fosters a harmonious environment by fostering strong connections between team members. This, in turn, leads to increased morale, improved communication, and a stronger sense of trust within the organisation.

When to Use: This leadership style excels at fostering team healing, boosting morale during challenging periods, and building strong connections among team members.

Traits: Collaboration, friendly, relationship aware, empathy, conflict management.

Things to Note About the Style: This leadership style prioritises people and their well-being. Leaders focus on fostering positive emotions, team harmony, and a sense of connection within the team. Building strong relationships takes precedence over solely achieving tasks and goals.

---

[4] The New Leaders by Daniel Goleman

The Affiliative Leadership Style

Trust comes in two forms:

1. *Predictability Trust*
2. *Vulnerability Trust*

Predictability Trust

- *Sincerity*
- *Capability*
- *Capacity*
- *Consistency*
- *Care (Quality)*

Vulnerability Trust

The courage to:

- *Speak up without fear of retribution or ridicule*
- *Ask for help*
- *Admit mistakes*
- *Challenge others*
- *Give and receive feedback*

Chapter Reference: The Democrat

The Democratic Leadership Style[4]

Gives people a voice and ensures they feel heard.

Environmental Impact: *This leadership style, which prioritises listening to team member concerns, fosters a positive environmental impact. By creating a space for open communication (through one-on-one meetings and discussions), it keeps morale high. Engaged employees are more likely to be mindful of environmental practices and suggest innovative solutions.*

When to Use: *Leaders who use a collaborative style effectively facilitate discussions to reach consensus, ensuring everyone feels heard and their input is valued.*

Traits: Team work, collaboration, conflict management, influence, listening, empathy.

Things to Note About the Style: *Democratic leadership shines when a clear direction is needed, but the specific path remains uncertain. It's ideal for leveraging the abilities of a competent team to generate creative solutions and implementation strategies, even within the framework of a strong existing vision.*

---

[4] The New Leaders by Daniel Goleman

The Democratic Leadership Style

This approach should not be used in times of crisis and when urgent events demand on-the-spot decisions.

Checklists[7]

Checklists are an important tool. They come in two forms:

- **Do-Confirm:** *Pause and confirm completion of memorised steps.*
- **Read-Do:** *Complete tasks as you check them off.*

A good checklist is clear, concise, and focused on essential steps.

Team Debriefs: The After-Action Review (AAR) Process[8]

1. *What went well (and how can we repeat it)?*
2. *What lessons can we learn from challenges?*
3. *How can we improve our processes to achieve consistent excellence?*

---

[7] The Checklist Manifesto by Atul Gawande
[8] Extreme Ownership by Jocko Willink

Chapter Reference: The Commander

The Pacesetter Leadership Style[4]

As a result of its frequent misuse, a pacesetting style can have a highly negative impact on the environment.

Environmental Impact: While this approach can be effective for achieving challenging and exciting goals, overuse or misuse can lead to burnout and team discord. This happens because team members feel excessively pressured, resulting in a decline in morale.

When to Use: To get high-quality results from a motivated and competent team. This style works well with the visionary style and affiliative style.

Traits: Drive, high standards, impatience with poor performance, eagerness to dive in and take over, initiative.

Things to Note About the Style: This hands-on style is characterised by micromanagement, a hesitation to delegate tasks, and a tendency for the leader to take over from underperforming team members rather than invest in their development.

The continued high pressure can constrict innovative thinking.

---

[4] The New Leaders by Daniel Goleman

The Commanding Leadership Style[4]

As a result of its frequent misuse, a commanding style can have a highly negative impact on the environment. This is the least effective style in most situations.

Environmental Impact: *While the commanding style can be effective in emergencies by providing clear direction and reducing fear, it's generally the least effective approach for on-going situations.*

When to Use: *In a crisis, to kick-start a turnaround, or with problem employees.*

Traits: *Controlling, impatient, demanding, criticising, initiative, achievement, influencing.*

Things to Note About the Style: *By failing to connect individual tasks to a larger purpose, this style stifles a sense of shared vision. This disconnect leads to disengagement and a feeling of futility among workers, who question the very meaning of their work.*

---

[4] The New Leaders by Daniel Goleman

Chapter Reference: The Commander

The Commanding Leadership Style

Rooted in the rigid command structures of the 20th century, this leadership style is evolving in the modern military. Today, it often coexists and interacts with more flexible and collaborative approaches.

Traits to develop

- *Self-awareness*
- *Empathy*
- *Collaboration*
- *Feedback (effective and timely)*
- *Emotional self-management (lack of which can lead to micromanaging or impatience ... or worse)*

Other Key Takeaways

Success doesn't come down to how many resources you have but how resourceful you can be.

M.E.C.E. — Mutually Exclusive, Collectively Exhaustive. The traditional organisational structure that breeds siloed thinking[6].

---

[6] Team of Teams by General Stanley McChrystal

Pulling the Levers

When building a team it's important to build trust individually first, then with the team, before finally setting the vision.

1. Affiliative

2. Coaching

} Individual focus

3. Democratic

4. Visionary

} Team focus

Pacesetting

Commanding

} Only as needed

Chapter Reference: The Most Important Thing

Project Aristotle[9]

Project Aristotle is what Google called its research into what makes a high-performing team.

This is what they discovered:

- **Psychological safety:** This is the most important factor according to the study. It means team members feel safe to take risks, admit mistakes, and be vulnerable without fear of being judged or punished.
- **Dependability:** Team members can rely on each other to follow through on commitments and deliver high-quality work.
- **Structure & Clarity:** There are clear goals, roles, and plans for how the work will get done. Everyone understands their part and how it contributes to the bigger picture.
- **Meaning:** Team members feel their work is important and has a positive impact.
- **Impact:** The team has a clear sense of the impact of their work and how it contributes to the success of the organization.

---

[6] The Fearless Organisation by Amy Edmondson

Chapter Reference: The Most Important Thing

The Five Dysfunctions of a Team[10]

When a team runs into trouble the root cause can often be traced back to these five dysfunctions.

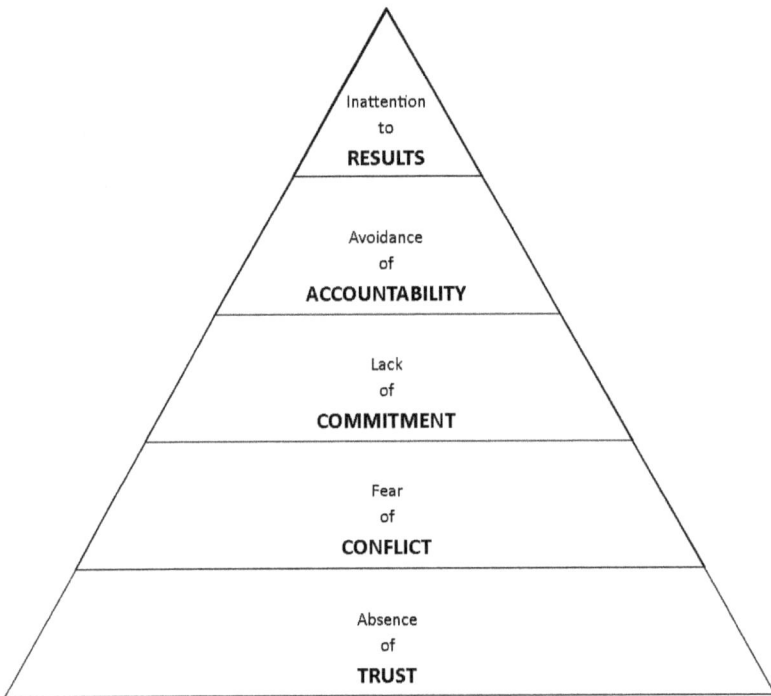

Inattention
to
RESULTS

Avoidance
of
ACCOUNTABILITY

Lack
of
COMMITMENT

Fear
of
CONFLICT

Absence
of
TRUST

---

[10] The Five Dysfunctions of a Team by Patrick Lencioni

Chapter Reference: The Most Important Thing

The Five Dysfunctions of a Team

Absence of Trust: This is the foundation of all the dysfunctions. Without trust, team members are hesitant to be vulnerable, share openly, or ask for help. This can lead to a culture of suspicion and politics.

Without vulnerability trust there can only be a sense of invulnerability, which creates an environment of fear and protection; an environment where mistakes are not accepted. Therefore, team members are likely to revert to poor behaviour such as hiding their mistakes or blaming others.

Vulnerability is essential for developing sincere relationships. First comes vulnerability, then comes trust.

Fear of Conflict: When trust is lacking, team members avoid productive conflict. They may hold back on disagreeing with ideas or approaches, even when they have concerns. This can lead to a lack of healthy debate and a feeling of inauthenticity.

Healthy conflict is essential for any high-performing team. Only through robust debate can the best ideas bubble to the surface.

Chapter Reference: The Most Important Thing

The Five Dysfunctions of a Team

However, the team must be mindful of not allowing debates to become personal; this is what can lead to unhealthy conflict.

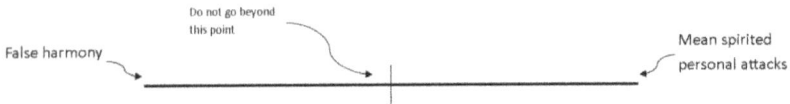

Do not go beyond
this point

False harmony

Mean spirited
personal attacks

A useful tool to ensure conflict remains healthy is to develop a team conflict agreement. An example of this might be:

We, the members of this team, recognise that conflict is an inevitable and even valuable part of a high-performing team. We commit to embracing healthy conflict as a catalyst for growth, innovation, and achieving our shared goals.

Our Values:

- ***Transparency and Open Communication:*** *We believe in open and honest communication, even when it involves disagreement. We will actively listen to each other's perspectives and strive to understand them.*

Chapter Reference: The Most Important Thing

The Five Dysfunctions of a Team

- **Respectful Disagreement:** *We value diverse viewpoints and will engage in respectful debate. We will attack ideas, not people, and focus on the merits of the argument.*

- **Psychological Safety:** *We will create a safe space where team members feel comfortable expressing their opinions, concerns, and even dissent without fear of judgment or retribution.*

- **Focus on Solutions:** *We acknowledge that conflict can highlight problems. We will use these moments to collaboratively explore solutions that benefit the team and the project.*

- **Commitment to Action:** *We will move forward with decisions, even if not everyone agrees entirely. We trust that open discussion has led to the best possible course of action.*

Chapter Reference: The Most Important Thing
The Reason We're in Business

The Five Dysfunctions of a Team

Lack of Commitment: Without healthy conflict and clear decision-making, teams can struggle to commit to a plan of action. Members may doubt the decisions made or feel uninvested in the outcome.

A lack of commitment leads to ambiguity. A large team is unlikely to ever reach consensus on important issues, therefore it's important to introduce this principle:

It's commitment we're after, not consensus

This approach can only work when the team has the opportunity to debate topics and feels heard.

Avoidance of Accountability: When team members are unwilling to hold each other accountable for performance or behaviour, standards can slip, and mediocrity can become the norm.

Inattention to Results: If the team is focused on individual agendas, personal success, or navigating inter-personal issues, they may lose sight of the overall goals and objectives.

Chapter Reference: The Three Outcomes

Giving Feedback

There are always three outcomes to keep in mind when giving feedback.

1. Seeking a change in behaviour or correcting a mistake
2. Clarity when delivering the message
3. Maintaining or enhancing the relationship.

Key Points:

The purpose of all approaches to feedback is to invite the other person into the conversation.

Look for opportunities to give praise. Remember to use the M.M.F.I. approach to interactions.

Make Me Feel Important

Chapter Reference: The Art of Giving Feedback

Giving Feedback[11]

The 3 phases of a feedback conversation are:

1. *Preparation*

2. *Formulation*

3. *Exchange.*

The preparation phase consists of:

1. *Understanding the **Outcome** you're after*

2. *Determining the **Action** you will take*

3. *Preparing for any potential **Obstacles***

4. *Preparing the **Solutions** for the potential obstacles.*

The different ways of formulating a feedback conversation are:

- *The feedback sandwich*

- *The You Choose approach*

- *The Outcome approach*

- *The Ask First approach*

- *The Next Time approach*

- *The S.B.I. approach.*

- *The I Statement*

---

[11] The ABCs of Effective Feedback by Rubin and Campbell

Chapter Reference: The Art of Giving Feedback

Giving Feedback

The steps for the exchange phase are:

1. *Own your own state*

2. *Deliver your feedback*

3. *Ask them what their thoughts are*

4. *Understand and empathise*

5. *Way forward*

6. *Inspire.*

Chapter Reference: The Man From Cork

Leadership Philosophy

The steps to developing your leadership philosophy:

1. *Determine your "actual self"*
2. *Determine your "ideal self"*
3. *Identify your strengths*
4. *Identify your gaps*
5. *Refer to the leadership style traits*
6. *List key words you use to define a great leader*
7. *Construct a statement using these words*
8. *Ensure the statement aligns with your "ideal self".*

Read this statement to yourself every morning to remind you how you want to show up as a leader. Allow it to influence your presence in meetings and the decisions you make.

And remember … "use your best judgement".

---

[12] The Leadership Challenge by Kouzes and Posner

Acknowledgements

I will forever remain humble because I know I could have less. I will always be grateful because I know I've had less.

~ Unknown

This book wouldn't exist without the teams I've worked with over the course of my career. My deepest gratitude goes to the head of my most important team, my wife, Louise, for your unwavering love and commitment to me and our girls, Sophie and Ciara. While murder and intrigue may dominate their current reading choices, I hope they'll discover the joy of reading one of my books someday. You both bring so much joy into my life.

To the man from Cork, Dr David Keane, who continues to generously share his wisdom and guidance without ever asking for anything in return.

To everyone who kindly offered to review this book before going to print; David Morrison, Darcy, Melsop, Colonel Mel Childs, Kirstie Knowles, Terry McCaul, Emma Parker, Yatish Parshotam and Anna Collins. I really appreciate your gentle critiques that have helped make the book more balanced and engaging.

I extend my deepest gratitude to all my clients and teams who have supported me throughout my career. Your challenges have fostered my growth, and your encouragement has fuelled my passion. It has been your invaluable contributions that have made this book possible.

Lastly, I would like to thank Barbara Unković, my editor, with her keen eye for detail, and for always turning things around in record time. Any writing mistakes are mine and mine alone.

Bibliography

We are like dwarfs sitting on the shoulders of giants. We see more, and things that are more distant, than they did, not because our sight is superior or because we are taller than they, but because they raise us up, and by their great stature add to ours.

~ John of Salisbury

Blanchard, K., Zigarmi, P., & Bunker, D. K. (2011). *Situational Leadership II: Effective Leadership Training and Development* (3rd Ed.). Pearson Education, Inc.

Collins, J. (2001). *Good to great: Why Some Companies Make the Leap...and Others Don't.* Random House Business Books.

Covey, S. R. (1989). *The 7 Habits of Highly Effective People* Simon and Schuster.

Covey, S. R. (1990). *Principle-Centered Leadership.* Franklin Covey.

Edmondson, A. C. (2018). *The Fearless Organization: Creating Psychological Safety in the Workplace for Learning Innovation, and Growth.* Wiley.

Gawande, A. (2009). *The Checklist Manifesto: How to Get Things Right.* Penguin Books.

Hearns, C. (2018). *First, Lead Yourself: Practical tools to unleash your leadership potential.* Setanta Consulting.

Katie, B. & Mitchell, S. (2002). *Loving What Is: Four Questions That Can Change Your Life.* Harmony Books.

Keane, D. (2012). *The Art of Deliberate Success: The 10 Behaviours of Successful People.* John Wiley & Sons Australia, Ltd.

Kouzes, J. & Posner, P. (2012). *The Leadership Challenge: How to Make Extraordinary Things Happen in Your Organizations* (5th Ed.). Wiley: Jossey-Bass.

Lencioni, P. (2002). *The Five Dysfunctions of a Team: A Leadership Fable.* Jossey-Bass.

Masterson, M. (2001). *From 6 to 7 Figures: The Ultimate Guide to Building Your Multi-Million-Dollar Business.* John Wiley & Sons.

McChrystal, S., Collins, T., Silverman, D., & Fussell, C. (2015). *Team of Teams: New Rules of Engagement for a Complex World.* Penguin Random House.

Peter, L. J. & Hull, R. (1969). *The Peter Principle: Why Things Always Go Wrong.* William Morrow and Company.

Rubin, I. M. & Campbell, T. J. (1998). *The ABCs of Effective Feedback: A guide for caring professionals.* Wiley: Jossey-Bass.

Scott, K. (2014). *Radical Candor: Be a Kick-Ass Boss Without Losing Your Humanity.* St. Martin's Press.

Sinek, S. (2009). *Start with Why: How Great Leaders Inspire Everyone to Take Action.* Penguin Books.

Willink, J. & Babin, L. (2017). *Extreme Ownership: How Navy SEALs Lead and Win.* St. Martin's Press.

About the Author

Cillín Hearns is a leadership and performance coach, author, trainer and team facilitator dedicated to helping individuals and teams achieve their full potential. With a unique background combining a Bachelor of Science in Applied Psychology and a Bachelor of Science in Computer Science, Cillín brings a blend of analytical and interpersonal skills to his coaching practice.

Cillín is the founder and director of Results Coaching, a company focused on empowering clients to enhance their leadership skills and overall performance capability. He is recognized as a leading coach in Wellington, having been named one of the Top 15 Coaches in the city in 2022. In addition to his coaching work, Cillín is the author of the book *First, Lead Yourself,* which delves into the importance of self-leadership for achieving personal and professional success.

Cillín's qualifications extend beyond his academic degrees. He holds formal certifications in coaching, that allow him to provide structured and effective guidance to his clients. This combination of education, experience, and expertise positions Cillín as a valuable resource for those seeking to unlock their potential and achieve their desired results.

Cillín lives in Wellington, New Zealand with his beautiful wife and his two lovely daughters.

To learn more about Cillín and Results Coaching, please visit www.resultscoaching.co.nz.

Results Coaching
Unleash Your Potential

FACILITATION   **TRAINING**   **COACHING**

Results Coaching is a New Zealand-based leadership and performance coaching company. Our mission is to empower individuals, teams, and organisations to achieve transformative growth and reach their full potential.

Focus on Results: Our core philosophy centres on achieving measurable and observable outcomes.

Leadership Development: We place a strong emphasis on leadership skills and believe everyone has the potential to be an effective leader.

Holistic Approach: Our coaching goes beyond just professional development. We recognise the importance of personal well-being and integrate this into our coaching programs, fostering a well-rounded approach to growth.

Values-Driven: We operate with the core values of passion, excellence, accountability, and creating a safe space for exploration, fostering a supportive and trusting coaching environment.

Whether you're an individual seeking personal growth, a leader looking to enhance your skills, or a team aiming to achieve greater results, Results Coaching offers a results-oriented approach to help you reach your goals.

RESULTS COACHING

For more information, please visit: www.resultscoaching.co.nz

First, Lead Yourself not only tackles the biggest problem in leadership development that holds millions of people back from achieving their full potential, it weaves together the essential ingredients required for your own success as a leader. This book is full of practical tools, exercises and insightful stories that will accelerate you along the path towards achieving your leadership goals.

Backed by research into personal change, high performance, resilience, and advanced communication skills, First, Lead Yourself is the perfect guide for anyone looking to step up and lead.

Part 1: Know Thyself - Develop Self-Awareness & Awareness of Others

Part 2: Bouncing Back - Develop Greater Personal Resilience

Part 3: Artful Communication - Advanced Communication skills that lead to better interpersonal outcomes

"Working with Cillín as my coach over the last few years he has taught me many, many tips, tricks, techniques, and strategies to inspect and learn about myself so that I can grow in my own leadership journey. This book is an amazing toolkit collection of those teachings and I for one am extremely grateful to have it all pulled together in one place. I can see that my own copy of this book is going to be well thumbed through and dog-eared before too long. Cillín's story telling and real life examples make this book memorable and, most of all, enjoyable to read."

June McClintock. Manager Products, FMG.

"This book is amazing. I had so many 'aha' moments. Although not really a self-help book, I've learnt so much about myself from Cillín. The wisdom Cillín shares has enabled me to become more resilient, a better leader, and most importantly, a better parent."

Luke Johnston. Director, Double-O Consulting

www.ingramcontent.com/pod-product-compliance
Lightning Source LLC
Chambersburg PA
CBHW030501210326
41597CB00013B/743